Exploring the Cumbia Family Tree

By

Samuel R. Whitby

Contents

Exploring the Cumbia Family Tree

Part 1

Research Report for the Cumbia Reunion in 2000

Oscar and Althea Cumbia, the author's maternal grandparents, in 1952

Beginning Research on the Cumbia Family Tree

Oscar and Althea Cumbia were my maternal grandparents. I grew up near them and knew them almost as well as I knew my own parents. Their lives and stories naturally became important parts of my consciousness, and they helped to form my view of the world. My grandparents especially influenced my understanding of family. One accepted fact was that my Granddaddy Cumbia was devoted to his parents. He remained close to his brothers and sisters. Knowing the importance of family relationships in the Cumbia family, including the ones between grandparents and grandchildren, I naively assumed that such sacred connections were the norm, if not in the world, at least among my kinfolk. I assumed that my Granddaddy Cumbia must have had a close relationship with his grandparents.

One day, while still a teenager, I asked my grandfather to tell me about his grandparents. He hesitated and then told me that he knew nothing about them. I asked if he could at least tell me their names. He looked puzzled and admitted that he did not know even their names. This struck me as strange. I believed him, but I could not understand how he could have grown up in a family that placed such emphasis on good family relationships without knowing anything about his grandparents.

Later, Granddaddy said he had thought more about my question, and he said he had been able to remember a few facts about the Cumbia family. He told me that his father, Robert Allen Cumbia, had grown up near Boydton, Virginia. Granddaddy said that he remembered one of his father's brothers, his Uncle John, a maimed veteran of the Civil War. Robert and John Cumbia had a brother who moved to Arkansas. They went to visit him one time, and afterwards they lost contact with him. Granddaddy added that he had met people named Cumby, and he believed that they were probably relatives. One of the Cumbys was a Baptist preacher named Mott Cumby.

Oscar had cousins, descendants of John, who lived near Smokey Ordinary, Virginia. Granddaddy took me to a store that was operated by one of those cousins, and he introduced me to his cousin. Granddaddy added that he remembered his mother's father, his Granddaddy Griffith, who near the end of his life lived in Brodnax with the Cumbias. When we attended a graveside service at Oakwood Cemetery in South Hill, Virginia, Granddaddy showed me the Griffith plot and the graves of some of his ancestors.

For a long time, the above was all that I knew of the Cumbia family tree. With a family reunion scheduled for October, 2000, I decided to do some research and to write an account of it for my relatives, hoping to communicate some of the excitement of discovery. At first progress was slow, but we did begin to learn about our family tree and history. I began to hope also to make the information available for future generations, so they could build upon our knowledge, without having to discover it all for themselves.

Readers with little time or patience will find a summary starting at page 131 and charts at the end of this book. This writer encourages readers to take the time to experience the thrill of discovery.

I have tried to minimize the use of footnotes, while adequately documenting my sources. Citing of vital records in most cases will refer to material at the Library of Virginia. Please consult the *Notes on the Cumbia Family*, soon to be available separately, if more documentation seems appropriate or necessary.

Since Grandmother Cumbia's death in 1993, I had kept the family Bible. In that Bible I found the birth, marriage, and death dates of many Cumbia relatives. There was also a mention of Great-granddaddy Cumbia's brothers: Willie, Jim, and John. Jim had been married to Emily Crow, and Jim had a son named John who married Chester Conner. In Great-grandmother Cumbia's handwriting there was a list of her relatives and their dates.

In the fall of 1999 the Church of the Latter Day Saints, the Mormons, began an internet page called Family Search.[i] The

Mormon page seemed potentially useful to people who wanted to look up their family tree. I checked to see the data on Cumbias, and I found several lists of people named Cumbia. The page gave names and dates, and it suggested questions. It did not, however, show the relationships between its data and the history of Oscar's branch of the family. Since then, I have learned that some of the Mormon page data are inaccurate, and one cannot accept findings reported on the Mormon page without verifying them.

My cousin Noel Cumbia became interested in the family tree, and he encouraged me to continue the research. He also looked up numerous internet resources that were very helpful. For example, he found that the Library of Virginia provided Internet access to pension applications of Confederate veterans and their survivors.

I followed up on Noel's discovery and found the application of Great-uncle John Henry. I also found the application of Emily Cumby, the widow of James Cumby.

Noel very helpfully pointed out that an Internet search on the name Cumbia would turn up mainly hits on a popular Latin-American dance called the Cumbia, and he suggested that a more efficient search could be made with the name spelled Cumbea.

Noel also found an Internet page that searched for residential addresses and phone numbers.[ii] We looked up Cumbias and Cumbeas using this resource. One day, acting on a whim, I decided to call a few of the people on Noel's list of Cumbias and Cumbeas. One of the first people I called was Dorothy Cumbea of San Antonio, Texas. She seemed completely delighted that I had called, and she explained that her husband, Charles, was a direct descendant of John Henry Cumbia of Virginia. We had a wonderful talk, and "Cousin Dorothy" said she would send me a copy of her research. She did, and her research is much of the basis for what we have learned about her branch of the family.

Dorothy pointed out that she had found relatives who spelled their names in different ways, such as Cumbia, Cumby, and Cumbie. I realized that I would have to broaden my search to include variant spellings and to establish relationships with more than just the same name. **In the account that follows, I will, when referring to a specific document, use the spelling found in that document.**

Dorothy mentioned finding that someone named Major Weatherford Cumbea-sometimes spelled Cumbia- had lived near Petersburg in the mid 1800s. (Major was his first name, not a rank.) Dorothy gave me her correspondence with a historian, Dr William Scarborough, who mentioned Cumbea in his study of overseers in the Old South. She also gave me her correspondence with Steve Cumbea's family, which was descended from Major Cumbea.

Using the Internet and email, I contacted Susan Lloyd and Steve Cumbea. Later, through Steve, I made contact with Larry Mills. Susan, Steve, and Larry are descendants of Major Weatherford Cumbea, who from 1845 to 1858 was overseer at White Hill Plantation, the Petersburg plantation that became the site of the Battle of the Crater during the War Between the States. Susan and Steve and I, and later Larry, carried on a lively and hopeful correspondence, but for a long time we could not establish a family connection. Later, we did discover that we were related.

Using Internet resources, I found the Census records for Mecklenburg County for 1850 and 1870.[iii] In 1870 a young man named Robert Cumby lived in the home of George and Pamelia Cumby. I was not sure that I had found the right Robert, the one who was my generation's great-grandfather. In 1870 there was a sister named Louisa, and in 1850 there were siblings named Ann Eliza, Mary, William, James, and John. In 1850 as a separate household there were Thomas Cumby, his wife Martha, and Cumby children named Lucy Ann, Louisa, and Green. Also in the household were Alex, Selena, and Martha Tucker.

Living near Thomas and Martha was the family of James and Catherine Pritchard (sometimes called Pritchett). Heartwell Arnold, a Methodist minister, lived in their household. The Morman page had already shown that Catherine was a Cumby. Later I learned that Thomas had given his consent for her to marry and signed a Bond agreement. Catherine was therefore probably Thomas's daughter. James and Catherine had children named James and Elizabeth. (See the section on Confederate war records for more about James.)

At about this time one of several lucky strokes of good fortune happened: I met, by email, Carolyn Davis. She was and is an expert on Mecklenburg County history and genealogy. She is also related to the Cumbys through Martha Curtis Tucker, Thomas Cumby's wife. Carolyn showed me that Martha had been called Patsy, and she pointed me in the direction of numerous useful documents. Carolyn gave me a guided tour of Mecklenburg County, showing me the final resting places of many of our ancestors.Her enthusiastic interest was an invaluable help in the research on the family tree.

I also had the great good fortune to meet by email Cindy Huggett, a descendant of John Henry Cumbia. Cindy has a sixth sense for genealogy, and she alerted me to numerous sources of information about our ancestors.

The Mormon page had several entries related to a James Wesley Cumbia. At first I believed that he was Robert's brother Jim. Several other documents indicated, however, that Jim was James Lewis Cumby, Cumbia, or Cumbea. The Mecklenburg County Marriage Register confirmed that James L. Cumby married Emily F. Crow.

I found on the Internet a map of Mecklenburg County in 1870.[iv] Section 7 of that map shows a Mrs Cumby's place, near Ebeneezer Church in the Buckhorn Township. Carolyn Davis has identified Mrs. Cumby as Martha Curtis Tucker Cumby. Carolyn pointed out that a state prison is now at the site of Mrs Cumby's farm. Martha was given the land by her father, Zacharia Curtis.

Dorothy Cumbea found a Brunswick County Marriage Register that identified the parents of John Henry Cumbia as James and Martha Cumbia. She gave that information to numerous people who passed it on. I have seen the Marriage Register, and it does list James and Martha as the parents of John. (Dr William M. Pritchett, in *Civil War Soldiers of Brunswick County, Virginia*, also identified

John's parents as James and Martha.[v]) Further research has shown that Dorothy's conclusion, based on one misleading document, was incorrect. According to the 1850 Census , James was only about four years older than John. Martha was the wife of Thomas Cumby. Among Dorothy's notes, I found a death certificate for John Henry Cumbia, and it identified John's father as George and his mother as Pamelia.

John's death Certificate revealed also that George was born in Campbell County, Virginia. Several other documents, including the administration of George's estate, confirm that George and Pamelia were the parents of Robert Allen and John Henry. Unshakeable family tradition establishes that John and Robert were brothers. Robert Allen's death certificate-strangely, a late (!) discovery-identifies his father as George Cumbia, with the information having been provided by Robert Ivan Cumbia, Sr.

The Census data – and later the death record- indicate that George Cumby was born in 1805.

Mrs. George Cumby was born in about 1814. Her name can be found spelled in various ways in different transcriptions: Permelia, Pamelia, and Pamela. I have seen the name in numerous handwritten documents, and it almost always has been spelled either Pamelia or Pamela. In the one case in which what seems to be Mrs. Cumby's signature is on a document, the name is spelled Pamela. I found her listed as Amelia in one document, so it seems likely that she pronounced it so that it would rhyme with Amelia.

I decided that it was time to make a serious commitment to research on the family tree, and I began to go to the Library of Virginia. The Library has many records on microfilm, where they are relatively easy – compared to traveling to court houses across the state – to find. (Also, the parking is free.) Documents at the LVA provided answers many questions about the family and its history.

The marriage record of Robert Allen Cumby and Mary Griffith identified Robert's father as Geo. A. Cumby. Nowhere, in any of the numerous documents that refer to George, have I found the "A" spelled out. A guess, due to the occurrence of the name in Robert Allen Cumbia and Robert's son Otis Allen, is that George was George Allen. John Henry also had a son, William, with the middle name of Allen. (There is an Allens Creek near the Kerr Dam.)

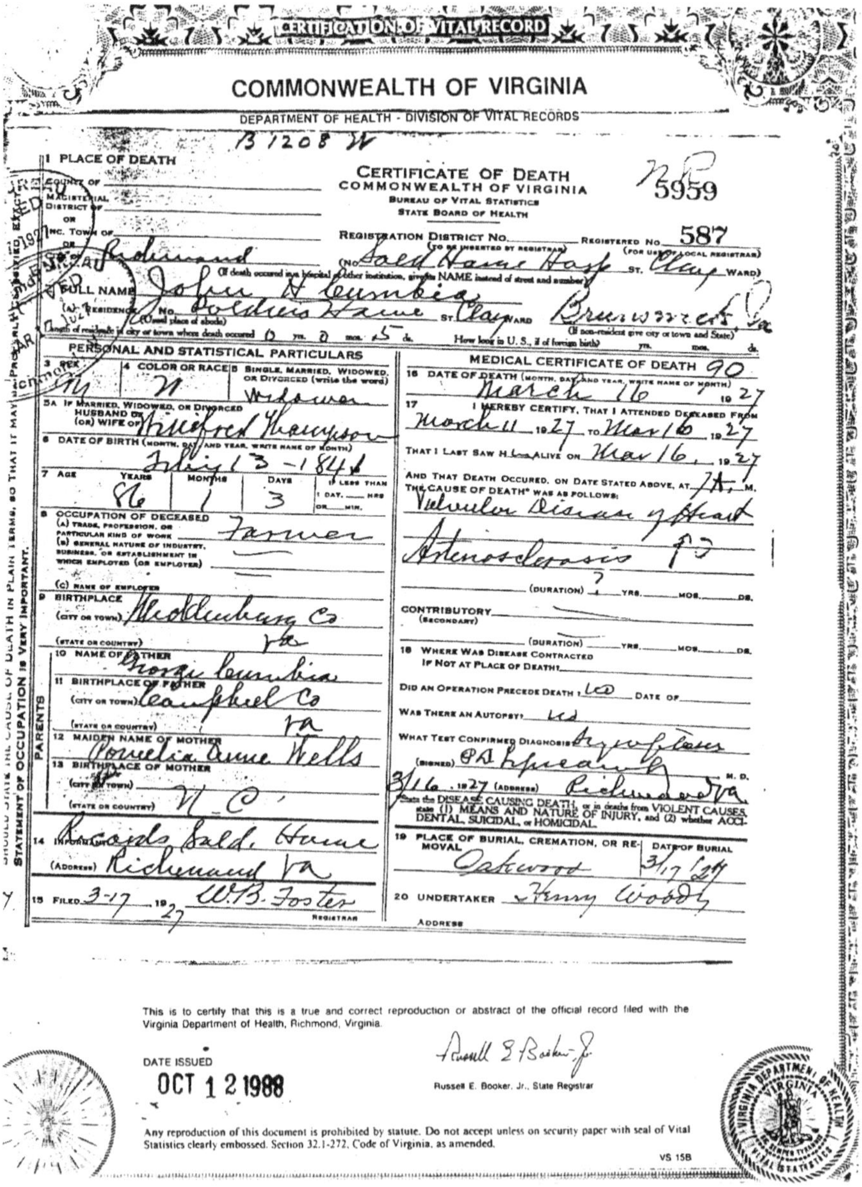

Figure 1.1 Death Certificate of John Henry Cumbia, provided by Dorothy Tilley Cumbea

Figure 1.2 Photograph found in the attic of the Robert Cumbia home place, believed to be a photograph of George Cumbia, provided by the author's mother, Louise Whitby

I also found the settlement of the estate of George Cumbia. His survivors were John, James, and R.A. Cumbia. (Paschal Cabaniss, a brother-in-law, was also a bondsman.) The families I had found on the 1850 and 1870 Censuses were the families of my ancestors. Dorothy's conclusion that James was John's father was incorrect, and as the research progressed, more evidence for this would emerge. Possibly James and Martha were witnesses of John's marriage, and they were mistakenly listed as parents. Maybe John and Winnifred "ran away" to get married, against the wishes of the parents, with the assistance of James and Martha.

George Cumby married Pamelia Anne Wells in 1834, not 1843, as the Mormon page had mistakenly indicated. George's Bond was $150. The written permission of her father, Henry Wells, is on microfilm at the LVA under Bonds and Consents.

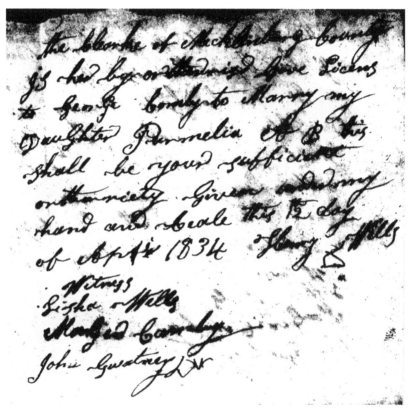

Figure 1.3 Consent of Henry Wells, found in the LVA. Note that one of the signatures seems to be Madj (as in Major) W Comby.

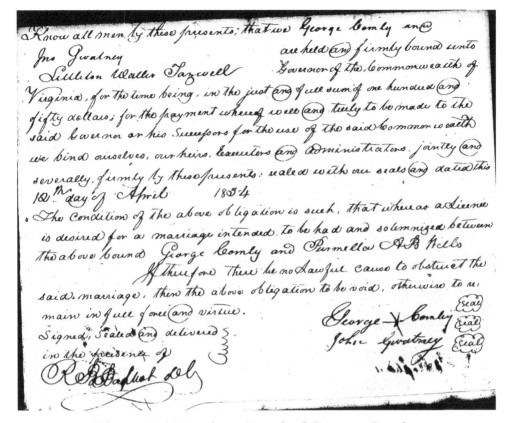

Figure 1.4 Marriage Bond of George Comby

I found Henry Wells' Will, which by itself is worth a trip to the Library. The Will identified Henry's wife as Mary and his children as Pamelia, Susan, Edward Lewis, Mary, and Harriet Early. Henry's parents, according to the Mormon page, were David and Susannah. There is a whole book about the Wells family, *The Wellses of Mecklenburg County, Virginia*, full of interesting information, in the Arnold Library in South Hill, Virginia. John Wells, one of the authors, generously sent me parts of the book. It includes photos of Pamelia's sisters, Mary and Harriet Early.

Figure 1.5 Photograph of Edward Lewis Wells, brother of Pamelia Anne Wells Cumby, courtesy of David Wells

The Marriage Register of Mecklenburg County indicated that one of Thomas and Martha's daughters, Lucy Ann, married George T. Morgan. They had twins who lived only one day. In 1870 Lucy and George lived with Martha in Mecklenburg County, and they had a six year old son named Edward. In 1880 Edward lived with Martha. George died in 1930, and his Will mentioned three more children, sons named George T., Jr., and Dr. Allen Morgan, and a daughter named Francis Morgan Wilson.

I have not been able to learn more about Thomas's daughter named Louisa. In Halifax County an unmarried Louisa Cumbie had a baby in 1872, and the baby died while still an infant. Perhaps that Louisa was the daughter of Thomas and Martha, but the record did not say. Perhaps George's daughter was mistakenly counted a second time, as a daughter of Thomas.

In 1837 George Combey agreed to buy the land that would become his family's farm. The sale was final on January 15, 1838. He bought 100.5 acres (called "be the same more or less") of the Tucker's Tract, paying $190.95. Although I have not located the precise site of George's farm, it was on Saffolds Road, not a great distance from Thomas and Martha's place.

Thomas Cumby married Martha Curtis Tucker, the widow of Robert Tucker, on October 7, 1839. If the 1850 Census data are accurate, in 1850 Thomas was 75 years old, and Martha was 41, so Thomas was 34 years older than Martha when they married. Carolyn Davis suspected that the age difference caused some problems with Martha and with Martha's Curtis relatives. The marriage must have been at least partly successful, for "old" Thomas sired four children with the widow Tucker.

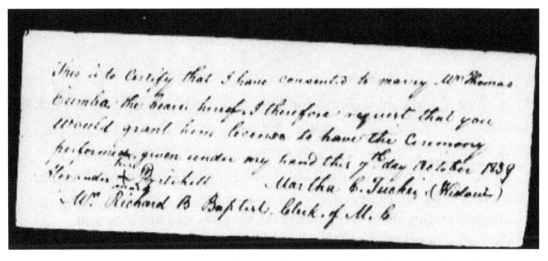

Figure 1.6 Consent for Martha Tucker to marry Thomas Cumba, from microfilm at the Library of Virginia

Catherine Cumby, probably Thomas's daughter, married James Pritchett (also called Pritchard) on August 19, 1839. Thomas gave his permission for her to marry. I did not find the Pritchetts in Mecklenburg County after 1850.

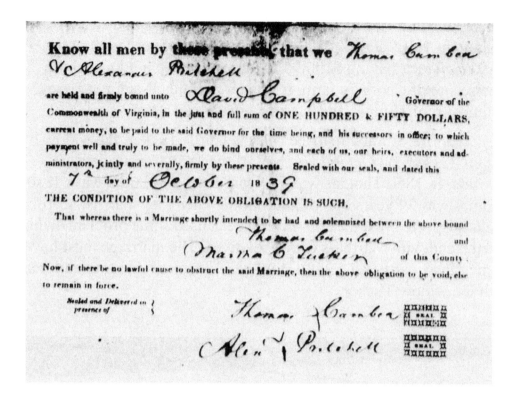

Figure 1.7 Marriage Bond for Thomas Cumbea and Martha Tucker, with Thomas's "X"

Having checked the 1850 and 1870 Censuses on the Internet, I looked for Cumbys on the 1860 Census at the Library of Virginia. Surprisingly, there seemed to be no mention of George Cumby's family. The Index at the Library of Virginia did not mention George's family either. The 1860 Census is very faded and hard to read, so perhaps the family is listed but cannot be read. There is also a family tradition, mentioned by Robert Ivan Cumbia, Sr., that some ancestors started to move out west. Finding the going too hard for them, they returned to Virginia. Perhaps George and his family started to migrate westward and were not counted in 1860 due to their migration. They were deeply in debt by the late 1850s, so they may have been trying to escape their economic situation.

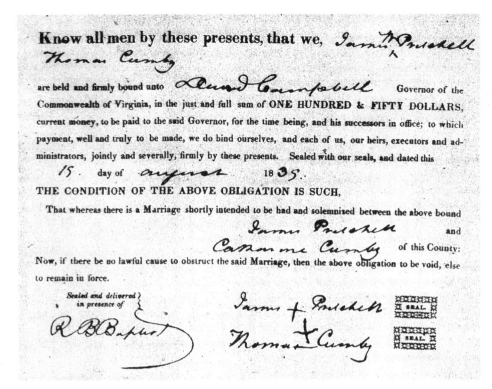

Figure 1.8 Marriage Bond of James Pritchett and Catherine Cumby

Figure 1.9 Prison at site of Mrs. Cumby's farm, photo by author

The 1860 Census of Mecklenburg County listed only two Cumbys: James, who lived with his aunts, Mary and Harriett Early Wells, and "Gnee" Cumby. Gnee may have been a mistaken rendering of Thomas and Martha's son, Green.

The Siblings of Robert Allen Cumbia

  Learning about the siblings of Robert Allen Cumbia has been a challenging but satisfying and fulfilling experience.

  Robert's oldest sister, Ann Eliza (perhaps Elizabeth), was born in about 1835. On September 15, 1858 she married Paschal Y. Cabaniss, and their family lived in Mecklenburg County near Ann's parents. The 1870 Census listed the Cabaniss family and five children. Ann's four sons were named William, John, James, and Robert C. - the same given names as her those of her brothers. She also had a one year old daughter named Gilbertha. I was saddened to learn that Robert, only five years old, died in 1872. (The Bureau of Vital Statistics reported the death in the wrong column, as five months.) The 1880 Census reported four more children: Gertrude, Walton, Asa, and L.A.

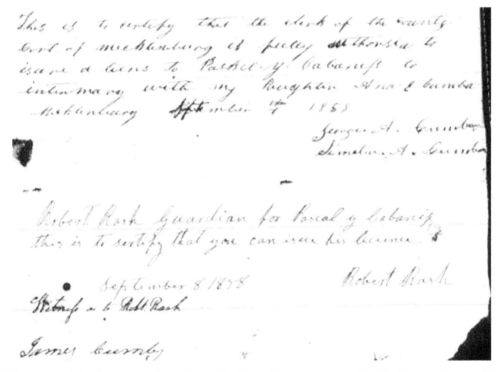

Figure 1.10 Consent for Ann E. Cumba to marry P.Y. Cabaniss, with James Cumby's signature, from microfilm at the LVA

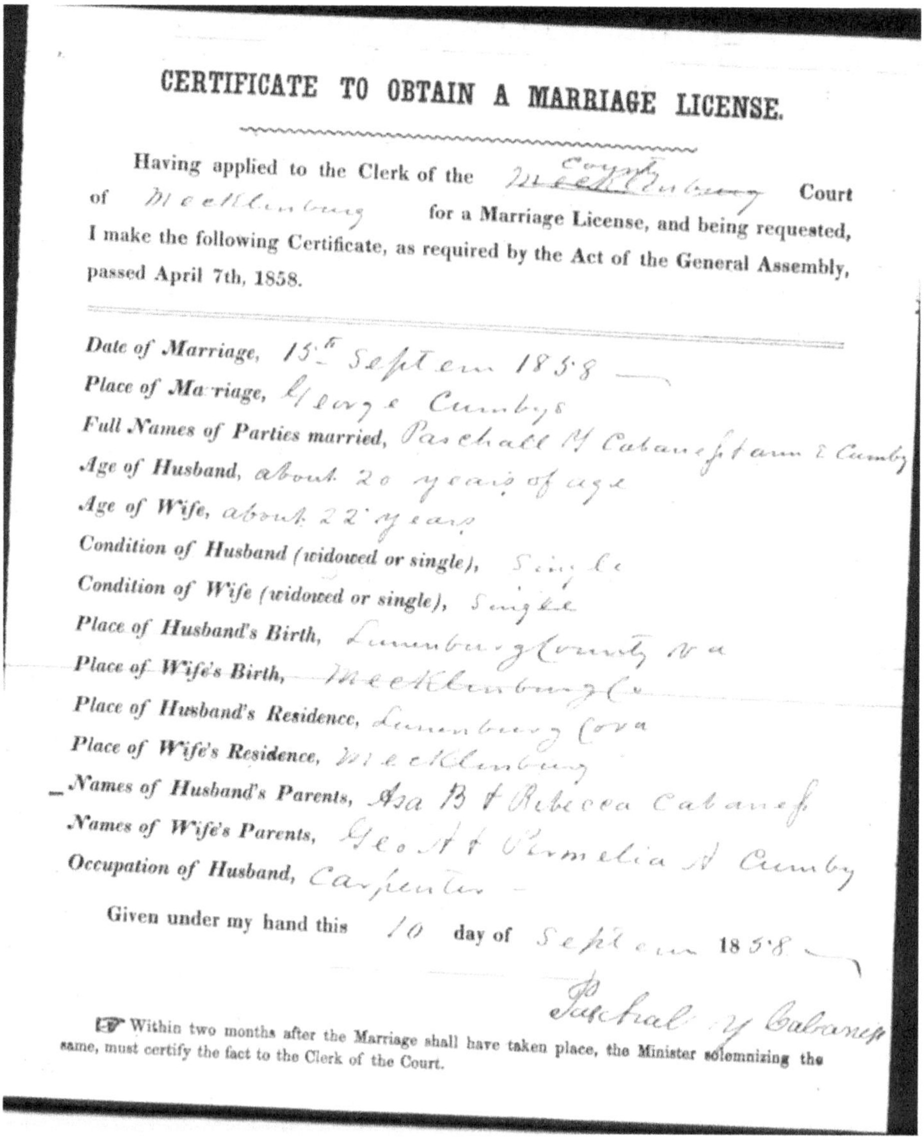

CERTIFICATE TO OBTAIN A MARRIAGE LICENSE.

Having applied to the Clerk of the _Mecklenburg County_ Court
of _Mecklenburg_ for a Marriage License, and being requested,
I make the following Certificate, as required by the Act of the General Assembly,
passed April 7th, 1858.

Date of Marriage, _15th Septem 1858_

Place of Marriage, _George Cumbys_

Full Names of Parties married, _Paschall M Cabaniss & ann E Cumby_

Age of Husband, _about 20 years of age_

Age of Wife, _about 22 years_

Condition of Husband (widowed or single), _Single_

Condition of Wife (widowed or single), _Single_

Place of Husband's Birth, _Lunenburg County Va_

Place of Wife's Birth, _Mecklenburg Co_

Place of Husband's Residence, _Lunenburg Co Va_

Place of Wife's Residence, _Mecklenburg_

Names of Husband's Parents, _Asa B & Rebecca Cabaniss_

Names of Wife's Parents, _Geo A & Permelia A Cumby_

Occupation of Husband, _Carpenter_

Given under my hand this _10_ day of _Septem_ 18 _58_

Paschal M Cabaniss

☞ Within two months after the Marriage shall have taken place, the Minister solemnizing the
same, must certify the fact to the Clerk of the Court.

Figure 1.11 Marriage Certificate of P.Y. and Ann Cabaniss

An interesting and very pleasing discovery was that a good
friend of mine in college, Kitty Cabaniss (now Katherine Cabaniss
Ph.D.), is a great granddaughter of Ann's son named John. Kitty's
father, Buford, remembers his grandfather, and he told me an
interesting story, told here with permission. John's main occupations
were millwright, blacksmith, and carpenter. As a sideline, given that

times were hard, he produced and sold some strong drink that once got him into trouble with the law. A roughly dressed man whose long beard was often stained with tobacco juice, John Cabaniss had a smart lawyer who advised him to dress up and to shave his beard. Cleanly shaven and neatly dressed, John could not be identified by the star witness, and he was found not guilty. John paid the lawyer with the forbidden beverage, and his lawyer said the wages were some of the best he had ever earned. Buford also remembers hearing the old folks talk about "Liza Jane Cumby." He remembers that they called her a "real frontier woman, who could farm and ride a horse as good as a man."

Figure 1.12 Tombstone of John Cabaniss

A sister named Mary was born in about 1838. I found a marriage record for a Mary Cumby who married John Kerr in Campbell County, and I thought that perhaps she was George and

Pamelia's daughter. The ages and dates did not, however, seem right, so I continued to look for information about Robert Allen's sister. Finally, David, my keen-eyed son, found a marriage record for Mary Susanna Cumby. She married David Gescoyn Brooks on October 19, 1865. She was 25, and he was 33. He was originally from England. His parents were John and Elizabeth Brooks. Mary's parents were listed as George and Pamelia Cumby. Mary married David in her father's home. Heartwell Arnold, a Methodist preacher, officiated. The 1870 Census showed Mary Brooks living with her aunts, Harriet and Mary Wells. She had two children, David H., 2, and Mary E., 1. I have tried, so far without success, to learn more about the descendants of David G. and Mary Cumby Brooks.

Another of Robert's brothers, James Lewis, called Jim in the family Bible, was born in 1836. In 1850 he lived with his parents in Buckhorn.

In 1860 James lived with his unmarried aunts, Mary and Harriett Early Wells. He served in the Confederate Army, joining on June 28, 1861, on the same day as his brother John. Jim served as an ambulance driver, transporting the wounded by wagon to field hospitals. After the war, he returned to Mecklenburg County, where he farmed and was a miller. Later, the family lived in Lunenburg County.

On November 30, 1865, James married a neighbor girl named Emily Crow (also called Crowe). The 1870 Census reported a one year old son named George A. In 1872 a daughter named Pamelia was born. In 1888 in Granville County, North Carolina, George married Jane Dunn (also called D.E. and Lizzie). George and Jane had sons named Walter and Henry and a daughter named Beulah. Walter died in November 1890, only ten months old. Beulah died from consumption in March of 1893 at the age of a year and four months. Henry died from measles on June 2, 1896, at the age of two years. George died from consumption on June 10, 1896, at twenty-seven. George's widow, Jane E. Cumbia, married J.E.J. Owen on September 15, 1897. One hopes that finally she had a happy life

Jim's father and Jim's oldest son both were named George A. Several researchers have written erroneous accounts of the family tree by failing to recognize that they were not the same person.

Jim and Emily also had children named Angelina, Major H., and John Robert. John married Sallie Connell (called Chester Conner in the family Bible), and they started a line of Cumbeas which survives in the Richmond area today. (Cumbea is pronounced with two syllables.) A daughter of Jim and Emily, A.S., probably (Pamelia) Angelina, died at nineteen in 1892. The 1910 Census showed Emily living with a 22 year old son named James Wesley.

According to tradition, related by a local man remembered as Mr. Farrar, James' Aunt Harriet Early Wells was a school teacher. Perhaps her relationship with James is one reason that James learned to read and write. The Consent for Ann E Cumba to marry Paschal Cabaniss is signed by James Cumby, and the signatures for George and Pamelia seem to be in James' handwriting.

In 1887 James agreed to support his Aunts Mary and Harriet Early Wells for the rest of their lives, in exchange for their part of the Wells land inheritance. The agreement between Jim and his aunts was extensive, meticulously listing the duties owed to them in exchange for the land. Jim agreed, for example, to yearly provide his aunts with 2 shoats for fattening, 2 barrels of flour, 3 barrels of corn, adequate pasturage for 2 cows and 2 horses, medical care, wood, hauling, plowing, and, if needed, a decent burial, among other things. When I first found the document, I thought at once that the demands on Jim were so excessive that the arrangement was unlikely to work out. Evidently the two elderly ladies were trying hard to provide for their old age, while aiding their nephew at the same time.

Mary died in 1887. In 1892 Jim agreed to pay Harriet Early Wells $250 for the land in exchange for his earlier agreement. Something must have gone wrong, for Jim and Emily defaulted on their agreement, with the result that the land was sold in order to pay Harriet her $250. A final settlement was delayed due to difficulty in surveying the property that had to be sold, and, when it was finally surveyed, the quantity of land was found to be substantially less than expected. (Photos of Harriet and Mary are in the *"Wellses..."* book.)

The 1880 Census showed James as a miller in Lunenburg County. According to Emily's application for a pension as a Confederate widow, James died of consumption on April 10, 1899. The 1910 Census showed Emily living in Chase City, with a son named James W., 26 years old. Evidently James W. was the James Wesley mentioned again and again, sometimes erroneously, on the Morman page on the Internet, as the husband of Corrina Tingen, and the father of a son, Alfred Earl. Emily Crowe Cumbea died in 1917, and she was buried in Mecklenburg County in the graveyard at the Crowe place.

Figure 1.13 Fred and Julia Cumbea, at the Cumbia reunion in 2000, photo by the author

Fred and Julia Cumbea, who live in Powhatan, Virginia, sent me a photograph of John Robert and Sallie Cumbea. John Robert had a darkly tanned face with a big smile under a huge mustache. Sallie, with a Connell family resemblance, also had a broad and winsome

Figure 1.14 Descendants of James and Emily Cumbea, photos
provided by Fred and Julia Cumbea

smile. Fred and Julia provided the descendants of John Robert and Sallie. They had sons named Robert Lee, John Lewis, Russell Rawlings, Walter Swanson, William Edward, Woodrow Wilson, and Gilbert Andrew. They had daughters named Clyde Davis, Ethel Catherine, and Nettie B.

Figure 1.15 Descendants of James and Emily Cumbea, photo provided by Fred and Julia Cumbea

Another brother, William, called Willie, was born in about 1843. There were no known records of his marrying or having children. I found a Confederate military record of a William A. Cumbia in Lunenburg County, and I thought this might be Robert Allen's brother. More research showed that his mother's name was Nancy, so he could not have been Robert's brother. Later, while studying Civil War records, I would learn more about William A. and more about the Willie from Mecklenburg County. (See pages 94-95.)

John Henry Cumbia was born in 1841. He served the South in numerous engagements during the War Between the States. He was wounded at Cedar Creek, where he lost three fingers of his left hand. According to his recollections as given to a newspaper on his eightieth birthday, he carried the South's colors at Kerrstown, Harper's Ferry, Fredericksburg, Chancellorsville, Spotsylvania Court House, the Wilderness, Cedar Creek, Gettysburg, Richmond, and Petersburg. He was with Robert E. Lee at the surrender at Appomattox Court House. John said that he tore the battle flag into pieces and gave it to his fellow soldiers rather than allow it to be taken by the victorious Northerners. According to family lore, John never got over his animosity toward the North. It was said that, when a "Yankee" salesman approached the house, John would go inside and shut the door.

Having returned to Virginia after the War, John married Winnifred Rebecca Thompson. Their children were named Laura, Charles Henry, Gracie, William Allen, Thomas Jonathon, Harriet Early, Minnie, Viola, John A., Annie Bertice, Emma, and Laura (there were two daughters named Laura), and Carrie. John farmed and reared his family near Smokey Ordinary, Virginia. John died on March 16, 1927, and he is buried in Oakwood Cemetery in Richmond. The Sons of the Confederate Veterans placed a stone marker at his grave.

Figure 1.16 John Henry Cumbia, photo provided by David Cumbia

Dorothy and Charles Cumbea
1996
"Our 50th Wedding Anniversary"

Figure 1.17 Dorothy and Charles Cumbea

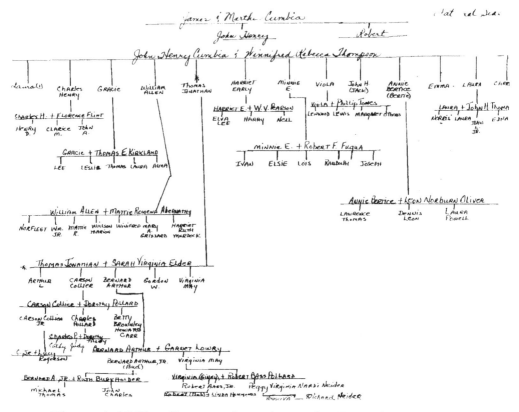

Figure 1.18 Family tree chart drawn by Dorothy Cumbea

The first Laura married R.D. Lucy. She died in childbirth in October, 1885. Charles Henry married Florence Flint, and they had children named John Albert, Clarice M., and Henry Darwin. Henry D very faithfully attended Cumbia family reunions. I remember a reunion held in the '70s, before which Henry arrived early, the first guest. Henry was well-known in Brunswick County as a former logger and enthusiast of family history. Several old family photographs which once belonged to Henry have survived his passing and have been given by thoughtful people to our generation. Gracie married Thomas E. Kirkland, and they had children named Lee, Leslie, Thomas, Laura, and Alma. William Allen Cumbia married Mattie Rowena Abernathy. They had children named Norfleet, William Junior, Mattie R., William Marvin, Winnifred, Mary A., and Harriet Ruth. Marvin ran a store at the crossroads locally known as Cochran, Virginia. Harriet Early (probably named after John Henry's aunt Harriet Early Wells) married W. V. Pearson. The Pearsons had children named Elva Lee, Harry, and Nell. Minnie married Robert F. Fuqua, and they had children named Ivan, Elsie, Lois, Randolph, and Joseph. Viola married Phillip Jones, and they had children named Lenwood, Lewis, Margaret, and others. John (Jack) married Ophelia Browder. Annie Bertice (Bertie) married Leon Norburn Oliver, and they had children named Lawrence Thomas, Dennis Leon, and Laura Powell. Emma and Carrie did not marry. The surviving Laura married John H. Thomas, and they had children named Norris, Laura, John H. Junior, and Edna. Cindy Huggett is descended from John Henry through Laura's branch of the family.

Figure 1.19 Harriett Early Cumbia, daughter of John Henry Cumbia, photo provided by Jeff Finch and Cindy Huggett

Dorothy understandably paid special attention to the ancestry of her husband, Charles. John Henry's son Thomas Jonathon married Sarah Virginia Elder, and they had children named Arthur L., Carson Collier, Bernard Arthur, Gordon W., and Virginia May. Carson Collier married Dorothy Pollard. They had children named Carson Junior, Charles Pollard, and Betty Brownley. Charles Pollard married Dorothy Tilley ("our" Cousin Dorothy), and they had daughters named Cathy and Judy. (Dorothy died on December 28, 2000.) Bernard Arthur married Garnet Lowry, and they had children named Bernard Junior and Virginia May.

Figure 1.20 Grave marker of John H. Cumbia, donated by the Sons of the Confederate Veterans, photo by the author

Robert's closest sibling in age was Louisa. Unmarried, only twenty one years old, she died from consumption on November 2, 1873. With a few exceptions (one of which is the 1850 Census record of Major Cumbia), her death record is the earliest known spelling of the family name as Cumbia. A photograph, from the attic of the home of Robert Allen and Mary Cumbia, has Louisa written in pencil on the back. My mother may have been named Louise in remembrance of Louisa.

I have found no confirmation that a sibling of Robert Allen moved to Arkansas and started a line there. Perhaps there was a brother who moved before the 1850 Census. I have been told that Great Uncle Burnice met Cumbys in Arkansas during his service in the Army. Perhaps the story arose from Burnice's visit. It may be simply a mistake.

Figure 1.21 Photo with Louisa written on the back, found in the attic of Robert Cumbia's house, provided by Louise Whitby

Robert Allen Cumby (later Cumbia), a great- granddaddy of my generation, was born on March 20, 1857. He was the youngest child of George and Pamelia.

Just when I was losing hope of learning more, I did learn more. I found Bureau of Vital Statistics records that an employee of the Library mistakenly had told me no longer existed. The Vital Statistics included the death record of George Cumba, with information provided by his son, R.A.Cumba. The Great-great granddaddy Cumbia of my generation died in September, 1884, at the age of 79. George Cumba's father was identified as Thomas Cumba. George's mother was not named.

Cindy Huggett, a descendant of John Henry Cumbia, had already correctly guessed the name of George's father. Carolyn Davis had written that she suspected it. Now there was firm evidence.

A big surprise was finding another death on a line above George Cumba's, the death of his wife, Lucy Tucker Cumba, who died the month before he did, on August 13, 1884. I was able to locate the record of George and Lucy's marriage. They married on December 19, 1872, with George identified as a widower. Evidently Pamelia Wells Cumby died sometime between being counted in the 1870 Census and the date of George's re-marriage. I was unable to find Pamelia's death in the death records of Mecklenburg County.

George Cumbia's cause of death was "tincture." This meant, perhaps euphemistically, death by alcohol. Having asked several experts in terminology, I have gotten no definite answer. My guess is that George, after the death of Lucy, drank himself to death.

Some Wells family members found and cleaned up a cemetery that seems to have been on the land formerly owned by Mary and Harriett Early Wells. At the cemetery there is a stone with badly eroded writing, which includes the date 1871. I think it is likely that Harriett's and Mary's sister, Pamelia Ann, is buried there.

At least part of the reason for Oscar Cumbia's lack of knowledge of his grandparents is now apparent. Granddaddy was born in 1902. His grandmother died in about 1871, and his grandfather died in 1884. He could not have known either of them. Still, one wonders why no one seems to have talked about them. I have learned that Robert Ivan Cumbia, Sr., knew the name of his grandfather, so the knowledge was available. Perhaps our ancestors were too busy living in the present to dwell upon or even consider the past. Perhaps there were dark or sad memories that were avoided by silence. I think it is likely that, by the time I came along to ask, Uncle Ivan had forgotten the name of his grandfather.

Figure 1.22 Photo found in attic of the R.A. Cumbia house, possibly
Pamelia Wells Cumby

Figure 1.23 Photo from Cumbia attic, possibly Lucy T. Cumba

Figure 1.24a Possible head stone for Pamelia Cumby, at Wells family cemetery, photo by author

Figure 1.24b Headstone with date marked and fossilized leaf imprint circled

Figure 1.25 Headstone placed at Wells cemetery,

Photo by author

Figure 1.26 Wells family cemetery, with Pamelia's stone on the far right, photo by author

George Cumby lived and farmed near his father and his father's new family. Green, Lucy Ann, and Louisa were George's half-siblings. (The 1860 Census listed another daughter, named Virginia. She appears on no other known records.) Green Cumby and George Cumby, half brothers, married Sallie and Lucy Tucker, who were sisters. Among the neighbors in 1850 were George's sister, Catherine, and her husband, James Pritchard. In 1870 the neighborhood included George's daughters, Ann Cabaniss and Mary Brooks, and their families, as well as James and his family.

As Robert Allen Cumbia's childhood ended, several troubling events occurred. Robert experienced a series of personal changes and losses. His mother died when he was about twelve years old. His sister, after whom my mother may have been named, died from tuberculosis in 1873. The War Between the States ended in 1865, when he was eight years old, and the South was defeated. The United States in 1873 entered a period of economic depression that lasted until 1877. The family farm was sold in 1875. In 1884 his step-mother died. His father died the following month.

When the time for the 2000 reunion approached, I started to expand the search by studying Campbell County records and began to accumulate data. Peter Cumby married Nancy Farthing in 1799, and Emmanuel Cumby married Molly Farthing, Nancy's sister, in 1800. In 1810 they paid taxes on 195 acres of land which had been part of the land patented to William Farthing, the father of their wives. Someone named Thomas Cumbo died in 1817, leaving a widow named Susannah. I made a list of Campbell County marriages of Cumbys, and the names are suggestive of family ties which we have forgotten: James, William, John, Kitty, Susannah, Nancy, Catherine, Lucy Ann, Eliza Ann, and Mary. All those individuals were Campbell County Cumbys, not individuals with the same names and who lived in Mecklenburg County. More information became known as research continued after the 2000 reunion.

36

The Children of Robert and Mary Cumbia

Figure 1.27 Robert Allen Cumbia and his wife, Mary Griffith

Robert Allen Cumbia (known locally as "Bob") married Mary Allen Griffith on December 20, 1882. The marriage license identified the parents of the groom as George A. and Amelia Cumby. Mary (known locally as "Mollie") was a daughter of Nathaniel Alexander Griffith and Sallie Francis Coley Griffith . She was born on October 16, 1857. I have found Mary's surname spelled in several ways: with and without an "s" at the end and as "Griffis" or "Griffin." The tombstones in the family plot at Oakwood Cemetery indicate that the name was spelled Griffith. (See Figure 1.32)

On the Sunday morning of May 27, 1906, Mary made a list of her family members, along with relevant dates. Her sisters were Emerline, Margaret Ann, Sallie Willie, and Nannie Aramanda.

She had brothers named Johnnie Alexander, Thomas Henry, and Joseph Albert Griffith. (See Figure 1.31)

Figure 1.28 Sallie Francis Coley Griffith, Mary Cumbia's mother

Figure 1.29 Robert Allen Cumbia and his wife, Mary Griffith, in
about 1930

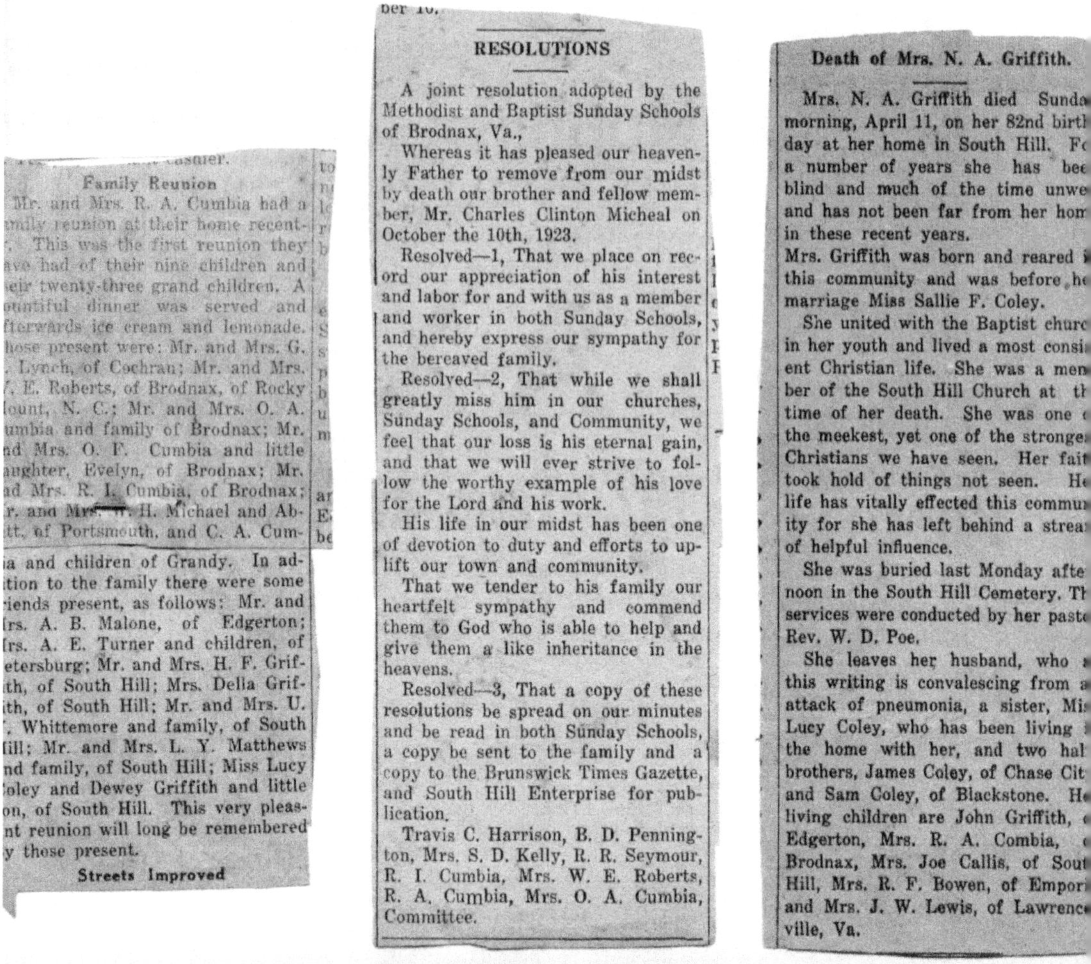

...cashier.

Family Reunion

Mr. and Mrs. R. A. Cumbia had a
amily reunion at their home recent-
. This was the first reunion they
ave had of their nine children and
eir twenty-three grand children. A
ountiful dinner was served and
fterwards ice cream and lemonade.
hose present were: Mr. and Mrs. G.
. Lynch, of Cochran; Mr. and Mrs.
. E. Roberts, of Brodnax, of Rocky
lount, N. C.; Mr. and Mrs. O. A.
umbia and family of Brodnax; Mr.
nd Mrs. O. F. Cumbia and little
aughter, Evelyn, of Brodnax; Mr.
ad Mrs. R. I. Cumbia, of Brodnax;
r. and Mrs. ... H. Michael and Ab-
tt, of Portsmouth, and C. A. Cum-
ia and children of Grandy. In ad-
ition to the family there were some
iends present, as follows: Mr. and
Irs. A. B. Malone, of Edgerton;
Irs. A. E. Turner and children, of
etersburg; Mr. and Mrs. H. F. Grif-
ith, of South Hill; Mrs. Della Grif-
ith, of South Hill; Mr. and Mrs. U.
. Whittemore and family, of South
Iill; Mr. and Mrs. L. Y. Matthews
nd family, of South Hill; Miss Lucy
oley and Dewey Griffith and little
on, of South Hill. This very pleas-
nt reunion will long be remembered
y those present.

Streets Improved

ber 10.

RESOLUTIONS

A joint resolution adopted by the Methodist and Baptist Sunday Schools of Brodnax, Va.,

Whereas it has pleased our heavenly Father to remove from our midst by death our brother and fellow member, Mr. Charles Clinton Micheal on October the 10th, 1923.

Resolved—1, That we place on record our appreciation of his interest and labor for and with us as a member and worker in both Sunday Schools, and hereby express our sympathy for the bereaved family.

Resolved—2, That while we shall greatly miss him in our churches, Sunday Schools, and Community, we feel that our loss is his eternal gain, and that we will ever strive to follow the worthy example of his love for the Lord and his work.

His life in our midst has been one of devotion to duty and efforts to uplift our town and community.

That we tender to his family our heartfelt sympathy and commend them to God who is able to help and give them a like inheritance in the heavens.

Resolved—3, That a copy of these resolutions be spread on our minutes and be read in both Sunday Schools, a copy be sent to the family and a copy to the Brunswick Times Gazette, and South Hill Enterprise for publication.

Travis C. Harrison, B. D. Pennington, Mrs. S. D. Kelly, R. R. Seymour, R. I. Cumbia, Mrs. W. E. Roberts, R. A. Cumbia, Mrs. O. A. Cumbia, Committee.

Death of Mrs. N. A. Griffith.

Mrs. N. A. Griffith died Sunda
morning, April 11, on her 82nd birth
day at her home in South Hill. Fo
a number of years she has bee
blind and much of the time unwe
and has not been far from her hom
in these recent years.
Mrs. Griffith was born and reared i
this community and was before he
marriage Miss Sallie F. Coley.

She united with the Baptist churc
in her youth and lived a most consi
ent Christian life. She was a mem
ber of the South Hill Church at th
time of her death. She was one o
the meekest, yet one of the stronge
Christians we have seen. Her fait
took hold of things not seen. He
life has vitally effected this commu
ity for she has left behind a strea
of helpful influence.

She was buried last Monday afte
noon in the South Hill Cemetery. Th
services were conducted by her past
Rev. W. D. Poe.

She leaves her husband, who a
this writing is convalescing from a
attack of pneumonia, a sister, Mi
Lucy Coley, who has been living i
the home with her, and two hal
brothers, James Coley, of Chase Cit
and Sam Coley, of Blackstone. He
living children are John Griffith, o
Edgerton, Mrs. R. A. Combia, o
Brodnax, Mrs. Joe Callis, of Sout
Hill, Mrs. R. F. Bowen, of Empor
and Mrs. J. W. Lewis, of Lawrence
ville, Va.

Figure 1.30 Newspaper clippings found in the family Bible, including the obituary of Sallie Griffith

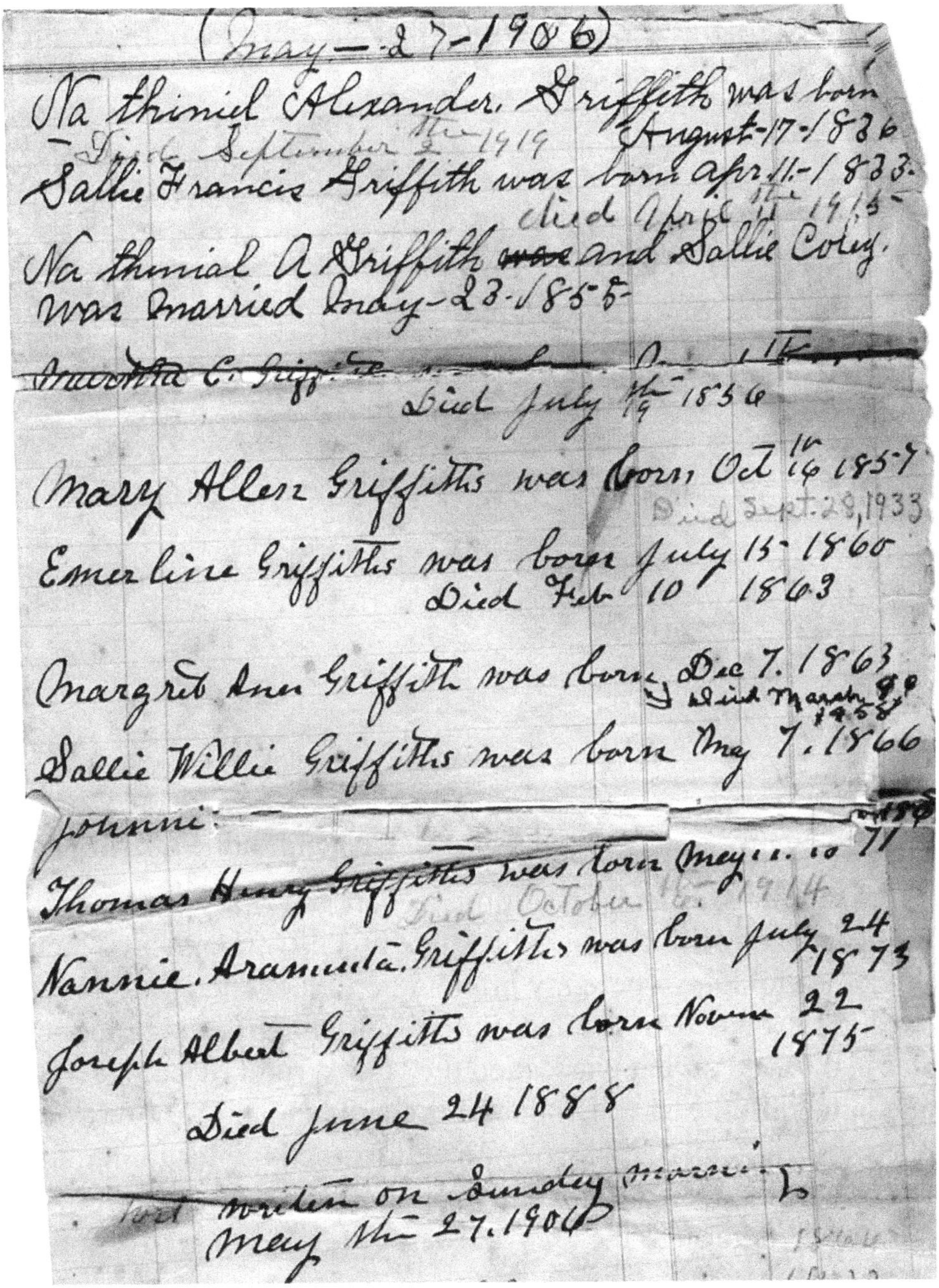

(May — 27-1906)

Na thiniel Alexander Griffith was born
~~Died September the 1919~~ August-17-1836
Sallie Francis Griffith was born apr 11-1833
died April the 1915
Na thinial A Griffith ~~was~~ and Sallie Coley
was married May-23-1855

Maratha C. Griffith ~~was~~
died July 7th 1856

Mary Allen Griffiths was born Oct 16 1857
Died Sept. 29, 1933

Emerline Griffiths was born July 15- 1860
Died Feb 10 1863

Margret Ann Griffith was born Dec 7. 1863
died March 8th 1868

Sallie Willie Griffiths was born May 7. 1866

Johnnie

Thomas Henry Griffiths was born May 10 71
Died October 16 1914

Nannie. Aramenta. Griffiths was born July 24 1873

Joseph Albert Griffitts was born Novem 22 1875

Died June 24 1888

was written on Sunday morning
May the 27. 1906

Figure 1.31 Mary Allen Griffith Cumbia's handwritten list of her
relatives, with pencil additions by Althea Cumbia, found in the
Cumbia family Bible

Sallie Griffith's Will specified that she must be buried with a headstone with her Vital data on it.

Figure 1.32 Graves of Nathanial (front, left) and Sallie Griffith(r.)

According to family tradition, Robert and Mary Cumbia first lived near South Hill. A man who knew Oscar Cumbia when he was a child once told me where my grandfather lived when the Cumbias moved to Brodnax. Mr. Emmett Pulley, a lifelong friend, told me that Oscar had lived in what was called the "old Wright place." It was immediately southeast of Brodnax Lumber Company, known locally as the saw mill, on Highway 58. When I learned the location, in the early '70s, the place had been cut over and had a new growth of trees. I walked through the area and saw the foundation of a house and the remains of a well.

In 1911 Robert and Mary purchased from R.R. Jones about 90 acres of the Northington Tract, the first section of the farm in Brodnax, where they lived for the rest of their lives. Their house was originally only one story. Oscar, Sr., liked to tell how it began to rain for days after they removed the roof to add a second story to the house.

When my grandfather was a child, his father, Robert Allen, wore a beard. Granddaddy remembered, on the day his father shaved his beard, asking his mother who was that strange man in the house.

Robert Allen was a farmer, and Evelyn and Louise, Robert's grandchildren, fondly remembered their grandfather's cultivation of fruit and vegetables. They have told me that he, a tobacco farmer, also grew strawberries, raspberries, apples, and pears. He planted asparagus, with descendants that still grow wild on the farm. I am pleased to have been able to transplant into my garden asparagus crowns that began with his garden almost a century ago.

Granddaddy would occasionally quote sayings of his father. He liked to say that his father advised to "never put off until tomorrow the work that you can do today." He argued that "a thing worth doing at all is a thing worth doing well." He also liked to say that "early to bed and early to rise makes a man healthy, wealthy, and wise." Evidently Robert Allen was taught some of the sayings of Ben Franklin's Poor Richard.

Grandmother, Althea Woodall Cumbia, remembered that "Mr. and Ms. Cumby" welcomed her into the family and that Mr. Cumbia had a lively sense of humor.

Evelyn remembers that her grandfather was the unofficial dentist of the neighborhood. If a neighbor needed a tooth pulled, Bob Cumbia was the one to pull it. He had a special tool, a sort of pair of pliers, with which he would pull an offending tooth. One can imagine that, in the days before effective anesthesia, Bob Cumbia's extraction of a tooth was an unforgettable experience.

Cousin David Cumbia recalls hearing that Bob Cumbia in his later years enjoyed taking trips on the train.

Evelyn remembers that her grandmother always made her feel special. She would sit on the floor and play with her, while wearing a long, heavy dress that was typical of women of her age at that time.

She made Evelyn's favorite meal of cornbread and turnip greens for her.

Evelyn remembers "gettin' a switchin'" from her mother, after she disobeyed her and went to see her grandmother without permission.

Mary Cumbia's obituary, which we have unfortunately lost, mentioned that she had attended Randolph-Macon College.

Robert and Mary were early members of Sanford Memorial Baptist Church, and their children are listed among the charter members. Earlier, according to Oscar Senior, they had attended the Christian Church in South Hill.

Mary died on September 18, 1933. Robert Ivan Cumbia, Jr., said that he remembered his grandmother's funeral. Her coffin was at the home place, and the pallbearers, her sons, carried it outside and then once around the house before walking with it to the cemetery. Robert Allen died on March 8, 1935. On their gravestones, in the family cemetery in Brodnax, one can read that "Dying is but going home" and "There are no partings in Heaven."

Figure1.33 Tombstone of Robert and Mary Cumbia

Robert and Mary Cumbia had nine children, all but two of whom I knew personally. They were Mamie, Charlie, Sue, Ivan, Dessie, Otis, Burnice, David, and Oscar.

Figure 1.34 Eddie and Mamie Roberts

Robert and Mary's first child, Mamie, was born on November 9, 1883. Mamie lived in Brodnax, Virginia. She married W.E. (Eddie) Roberts on December 14, 1904. Uncle Eddie and Aunt Mamie had a farm that was on the western border of the Cumbia home place farm. Uncle Eddie was a very active and loyal member of the Woodmen of the World. Extremely afraid of being immersed in water, Uncle Eddy remained a member of the Methodist Church, while regularly, with Mamie, attending the local Baptist church. Although he died when I was only a small boy, I remember him as a thin man with a moustache. Aunt Mamie taught Sunday school at

Sanford Memorial Baptist Church for many years. Aunt Mamie and Uncle Eddie had no biological children, but they had two foster children, a daughter named Beatrice and a son named Tommy. (Tommy told me that, no matter who had given birth to him, Mrs. Roberts, Aunt Mamie, was his *real* mother.) They also assisted with the rearing of the children of Mamie's brother, Charlie, after he died. Late in her life Aunt Mamie developed severe memory loss that today would probably be diagnosed as Alzheimer's disease, and she died in June, 1970.

Charlie Cumbia was born on March 1, 1885. He married Hattie Hightower on July 24, 1910. They lived near Grandy, Virginia, and they had children named Herbert, Alma May, Charles Allen (known as Allen), Thomas Jefferson (called Jeff), and Florence. Charlie Cumbia had heart problems due to kidney disease, and he became unable to work. Robert Allen had a house built on the family farm, in order that Charlie's family might come to live there, but Charlie did not live long enough for them to move in. He died on March 20, 1928. Alma Cumbia married Clifton Baird, and they lived in Brodnax, almost in sight of the Robert and Mary Cumbia home place.

Figure 1.35 Charlie Cumbia, photo courtesy of Kenny Michael

Figure 1.36 Charlie Cumbia and (girlfriend?) Queen Roberts, photo courtesy of Kenny Michael

Figure 1.37 Charlie and Hattie Cumbia and their son Allen

Figure 1.38 Charlie and Hattie Cumbia's sons

Anna Bell Cumbia (usually called Sue) was born on October 23, 1886. She married G. E. Lynch on September 6, 1908. They had one child who died as a baby. My mother remembered that someone once left a baby on Aunt Sue's doorstep, evidently picking Sue and "Mr. Lynch"-which is what Aunt Sue called her husband- as good foster parents. Aunt Sue took the baby to their equivalent of what we would call Social Services. She "took in" Allen Cumbia after Charlie died. Aunt Sue was the cook at Brodnax Elementary School when my mother was a child. After the death of Mr. Lynch, Aunt Sue married Floyd Dawson, a brother of Aunt Josie and Aunt Bessie, a very kind, friendly man who I remember well, for he would take time with children. He liked to tell funny stories. Uncle Floyd was a widower with a child, and Aunt Sue called her second husband Daddy. Aunt Sue died on September 3, 1958, one day after her brother, Burnice. Dr. William Pritchett mistakenly identified Anna Belle Cumbia as a daughter of John Henry Cumbia.

Figure 1.39 Anna Bell (Sue) Cumbia Lynch Dawson

Robert Ivan Cumbia, Sr., was born on November 1, 1888. He married Bessie Dawson on January 12, 1908. They lived in Brodnax and farmed. They had sons named Alpheus Thomas, Wilford Garner, and Robert Ivan, Jr, and daughters named Hortense and Elwood. Uncle Ivan faithfully attended Sanford Memorial Baptist Church, and his pond was used for baptisms. One of the fields on Ivan's farm was designated, during World War Two, as an emergency landing strip, thereby becoming, one could say, the first airport in Brodnax. My father remembered finding Uncle Ivan looking at the sunset. Uncle Ivan explained that he was just sitting there and thinking about how beautiful Heaven must be. He was a very kind, soft-spoken man who enjoyed taking Oscar's grandchildren fishing with him. He loved animals, and he seemed to have a special place in his heart for stray dogs. He adopted one of my hounds that liked to roam, and he took care to feed the dog well. Several times in the '60s, when we were fishing, Uncle Ivan with a trembling voice told me that his wife had been a very good woman and that he had never stopped missing her. He always spoke of Aunt Bessie with feeling. Robert Ivan, Sr., died on August 24, 1972.

Figure 1.40 Robert Ivan Cumbia, Senior

When Robert Allen Cumbia died, all of his children except Ivan agreed to sell their interest in the farm to the youngest brother, Oscar, my grandfather. When Aunt Bessie became ill, Uncle Ivan decided that he must sell his interest in order to pay for her medical care. These circumstances caused some hard feelings in the family for awhile. By the time that I came along, Oscar and Ivan had put this issue long behind them, and they shared a very deep friendship.

Figure 1.41 Ivan and Bessie Cumbia and family, photo courtesy of Darlene Hinman

Figure 1.42 Uncle Ivan's pond, photo courtesy of Darlene Hinman

Dessie D. Cumbia was born on November 16, 1891. She married W.H. (Harry) Michael on December 27, 1916. Uncle Harry ran a gas station that was near the Brodnax United Methodist Church. During World War Two there was an air raid warning building with a telephone behind the station, and every airplane that passed over had to be reported to the authorities. Uncle Harry was remembered for often calling to Aunt Dessie, "Pote it [report it]." Dessie and Harry had one child who died as a baby, and they had a son named Abbitt who was a favorite visitor at Oscar's place. Aunt Dessie was well known and beloved among her nieces and nephews for her friendliness and her sense of humor. (One time she took someone up on a dare and bit the head off a tobacco worm.) Aunt Dessie liked to joke that the "D" in Dessie D stood for devil. (She was Des Demona Cumbia.) She enjoyed recalling that, while Mamie and Eddie were getting married, Oscar had been a toddler in her arms. Oscar disturbed the solemnity of the occasion by begging for a drink of water. Aunt Dessie related that she was responsible for the spelling of the family name as Cumbia. Although I have found that spelling as early as 1850, I think that she probably did persuade the rest of the family to use her spelling. The tradition has been that she changed the spelling on a whim, and her personality was so attuned to humor that one finds it easy to believe the tradition. Aunt Dessie died on August 4, 1974.

Figure 1.43 Dessie, Oscar, and Sue

MICHAELS Tire & Battery Station

W. H. MICHAEL, of Michael's
Tire & Battery Station.

APRIL 1948

Figure 1.44 Uncle Harry Michael and the service station, photo
courtesy of Kenny Michael

Figure 1.45 Abbitt Michael and goat cart, photo courtesy of Kenny
Michael

Otis Allen Cumbia was born on December 6, 1893. He married Josie Dawson, the sister of Ivan's wife. Otis and Josie had fraternal twins named Jesse and Philip, sons named Otis Douglas and Joseph Lester, and a daughter named Naomi. Aunt Josie taught Sunday school at Sanford Memorial Baptist Church. She was my first Sunday school teacher. Uncle Otis was a Town Council member in Brodnax. Uncle Otis was a soft -spoken man, who seldom raised his voice above a whisper. He had a farm on the edge of Brodnax and another farm known locally as the Bridge Plantation, so named for its proximity to a bridge over the Meherrin River. (Later research would show other relatives-Gideon Cumbo and Thomas Cumby- who owned farms along the Meherrin.) Uncle Otis was a well-driller, a plumber, and an electrician. He wired Oscar's and Althea's house for a Delco electric generator, back in the days when the Rural Electrification Project had not yet put power lines in rural Virginia, with the foresight to wire also for alternating current, in anticipation

Figure 1.46 Otis Cumbia and Dessie Michael, among the worshipers at Sanford Memorial Baptist Church

of the coming power lines. My grandfather told me he thought that Otis was the smartest man he had ever known. He said that Otis could repair almost anything, and if he could not repair something, he could build a new one. One day, near the end of Uncle Otis's life, after he had already lost a leg to diabetes, I saw him make a gasket by cutting a piece of cork with his pocket knife. Otis and Oscar had a barber shop in Brodnax during the thirties, and they would cut hair on Friday nights and Saturdays. One of my oldest memories is of Otis and Oscar taking turns cutting each other's hair on the back porch. Otis died on February 11, 1967.

Figure 1.47 Congregation at SMBC, with Josie Dawson Cumbia on right, wearing a dark hat

George Burnice Cumbia was born on August 18, 1895. He married Bertha Holton on December 27, 1916. They had children named Robert, Clifton, George Burnice, Jr., Martha, Elizabeth, Mary, and Bernice. Uncle Burnice was a veteran of World War One. He had an automobile repair shop, called the garage, in Portsmouth, Virginia. Oscar's family found it noteworthy that Burnices's family subsisted on two meals a day, one in the late morning and another at around three in the afternoon. Burnice insisted that the first course of the afternoon meal would be dessert. Oscar's daughters, Evelyn and Louise, have told that they very much enjoyed the summer visits of their cousins from Portsmouth. Aunt Bertha especially enjoyed visiting Aunt Dessie. Burnice enjoyed deer hunting with Oscar, and Oscar enjoyed duck hunting with Burnice. Uncle Burnice died from cancer on September 2, 1958.

Figure 1.48 Burnice Cumbia, photo courtesy of Kenny Michael

Figure 1.49 George Burnice and Bertha Cumbia

Figure 1.50 Burnice Cumbia at his garage, photo courtesy of Robert and Gloria Cumbia

 Clarence David Cumbia, Sr., usually called David, was born on September 9, 1899. He married Richlee Harrison on February 20, 1918. They had children named Margie Louise, Mary Elizabeth, Robert (Bobby), Clarence, and Vernon. After the death of Richlee, David married Elsie. David lived in Rocky Mount, North Carolina, and he worked on the railroad. Like many other families, David's family had a hard time during the Great Depression, with layoffs being a source of worry. When laid off from the railroad, David drove an oil truck. After his death, some of David's children lived for awhile in an orphanage in North Carolina. David died on November 2, 1935.

Figure 1.51 Clarence David Cumbia, Sr

Figure 1.52 Ritch Lee and Bertha Cumbia

Oscar Francis Cumbia, my grandfather, was born on January 15, 1902. He married Althea Gaines Woodall on August 4, 1924. They had children named Evelyn Mary, Edna Louise, and Oscar Francis, Jr. A kind, soft -spoken man, Oscar was a farmer and part-time barber. He made delicious stews, and he customarily cooked a large stew for the opening of a tobacco market in South Hill. Several times advertisements with Oscar's photo and testimonial were published in agricultural magazines. Oscar was well known locally as a grower of watermelons and cantaloupes. He liked to hunt and fish, and late in his life he enjoyed fishing with his grandchildren.

There were also some dark realities that cast shadows on the family's happiness. Grandmother conceived another child, a male, who died when there were complications with the pregnancy, and Grandmother almost died from blood loss. Early in his life, at 35, Granddaddy learned that he had an inoperable, life-threatening aneurism, and he lived and worked for the rest of his life with the knowledge that his life might be a short one. Through the difficult years of the Great Depression, Oscar worked very hard and sacrificed many things, including his health, for his family. He would not have liked for me to have made a great deal of this. He would have said he had only been doing what was right. Oscar died on November 27, 1968.

Figure 1.53 Promotional photo of Oscar with Oscar Junior and
Louise in a tobacco field

Figure 1.54 Oscar, Althea, and toddler Evelyn

Figure 1.55 Ivan, Dessie, Mamie, and Oscar, at a Cumbia reunion in 1965

Figure 1.56 1927 Reunion, top: Robert, Mary (holding toddler
Evelyn), and grandchildren; bottom: Oscar (front); middle row, left
to right: Burnice, Robert, Mary, David; back row, left to right: Sue,
Ivan, Charlie, Mamie, Dessie, Otis

Part 2

Research Report for the 2003 Reunion

After the 2000 reunion, several goals remained. I wanted to learn the name of George Cumby's mother, and I wanted to extend our knowledge of our ancestors back even farther if possible. Another goal was to learn the relationship between Major Weatherford Cumbea and the Cumbias of Mecklenburg County. I wanted to establish the link between the family branches in Campbell, Halifax, and Mecklenburg Counties. Another objective was to learn where our ancestors were buried. I hoped to learn the source of an unusual genetic trait that had turned up in my family and the family of some Cumbia cousins. Some success, but not complete success, has been achieved in all these areas.

Thomas, Agnes, Major, and George

On the day after the reunion Cindy Huggett wrote that she had found a marriage of a man named Thomas Cumbey to Agnes Weatherford. They married on January 12, 1804, in Halifax County, Virginia. I was able to find the marriage records on microfilm at the Library of Virginia. We were unsure whether or not Thomas Cumbey was the person with that name who was a direct ancestor. Cindy also found several reports on Weatherford family genealogy. The name Major occurred several times. It seemed very likely, without convincing proof yet, that Thomas and Agnes were the parents of Major Weatherford Cumbea.

I chanced to learn that James and Emily Cumbea had a son named Major H. Cumbea. Reasoning that such an unusual name was evidence of a family connection, I more than ever became motivated to learn more about Major Weatherford and his connection to Thomas and George.

Searching records at the Library of Virginia, I found a death record for M. W. Cumbea. He died due to meningitis on May 10, 1872, at the age of 55. Major's wife, Adelia Hobbs, died the following year. The death record confirmed that Major's parents were Thomas and Agnes. It indicated that Major was born in Charlotte County. Charlotte County records show that a Thomas Cumby bought and later sold (at a hefty profit, over five times what he paid for it) land from Agnes's maternal grandfather, William Sublett. That Thomas had a wife named Susannah, and more will be written about them later. Steve Cumbea and Dorothy Cumbea had already told me the names of Major's parents, but I unfortunately and regrettably had overlooked that information.

Finding the connection between Major's family and George's then became a priority. George Cumba's death record did not identify his mother, and I at first despaired of ever learning her name.

Finally, I remembered that George Cumby's second marriage occurred after the County of Mecklenburg began to use marriage licenses, and I realized that a marriage license might tell the names of the parents. I found a marriage register that gave George's parents as "T & A Cumby." I searched for the Marriage License and found it. George and Lucy's license revealed that George's parents were "Thomas and Agnes his wife." George Cumby's mother was Agnes Weatherford Cumby, and George and Major were brothers.

I have not been able to learn a lot about Agnes Weatherford. The Halifax County Marriage Register indicated that she signed her own Consent to marry Thomas Cumby. One is inclined to imagine a young woman with some education and, as a Baptist in Anglican Virginia, a mind of her own. Regrettably, I have not been able to find her signature or learn when she died or where she is buried.

Weatherford family researchers have contributed to an interesting web page on the Internet.[vi] Citing their findings at length here would not be proper, but one bit of data that they report is widely known and accepted: the story of Agnes's father, Rev. John Weatherford. He was one of the early Baptist preachers in the colonies. Preaching as a Baptist during a time when the Church of England was the official state religion, Rev. Weatherford was jailed in Chesterfield County from 1770 until 1774. (The web page of the Chesterfield County Jail contends that those who jailed Weatherford were Presbyterians.[vii]) Ordered to stop preaching, he refused and preached to the jailors and to passers-by from the window of his cell. When he refused to stop preaching he was beaten on his hands by his jailors, receiving scars that lasted the rest of his life. Charged with preaching without a license, Weatherford was ordered to pay a fine. He refused to pay the fine, insisting that he had done nothing wrong, and he remained in jail and continued preaching, becoming something of a nuisance to the authorities in Chesterfield County. Someone, believed to have been his attorney, Patrick Henry, anonymously paid the fine and had him released from jail (to the probable relief of the jailors). Weatherford tried to reimburse Henry for the fine, but Henry refused to accept the payment.

The story of Reverend John Weatherford's imprisonment has been told and retold until it has become part of the religious history and Baptist lore of the United States. In Richmond the Weatherford Memorial Baptist Church, noted for the UVA-Rotunda-like architecture of its sanctuary and now part of St. Paul's Baptist Church, formerly was named for Reverend John Weatherford. A Memorial to Weatherford and several other early Baptist preachers is on the lawn near the old Chesterfield Courthouse and Jail.

Figure 2.1 Grave of Rev. John Weatherford, photo by author in 2003

Figure 2.2 Historical Marker near Weatherford's grave, photo by author

LeGrand Michaux Jones, in his memoirs, mentioned hearing Elder Weatherford preach when the preacher was in his nineties. He recalled that Weatherford "wore a knit woolen cap the whole time." He preached in a church where the white and black worshipers sat on separate sides of the sanctuary. [viii]

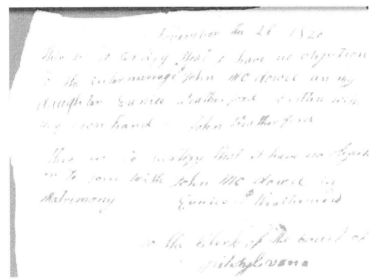

Figure 2.3 John Weatherford's signed Consent for his daughter, Eunice, to marry John McDowell

Figure 2.4 Weatherford descendants, David, Tyler, and Sam Whitby, at Chesterfield Courthouse, photo by Uta Whitby

Figure 2.5 My father, Ray Whitby, at Weatherford's grave in 2010

Major Weatherford Cumbea

Using LVA records and documents at the Virginia Historical Society, I was able to learn more about Major Weatherford Cumbea and his family.

"Major" is a name that is unusual but not unprecedented. It has been encountered, very rarely, in other families. There is a record of a slave named Major, and there are in Virginia today families with the surname Major. According to a Weatherford family researcher, there was a Major Weatherford who was either Rev. John Weatherford's father or his brother. Also, Thomas and Susannah Cumbee had a son named Major. In 1804 he married Margaret Mical in Charlotte County. Major Weatherford Cumbea could, therefore, have been named in honor of his grandfather (or paternal uncle), his maternal uncle, or both.

According to his death record, Major Cumbea was born in Charlotte County in about 1817.

Major was married at least twice. Reverend Daniel Petty's Minister's Return, dated October 13, 1835, lists Major's marriage to Nancy Morgan in Lunenburg County. Petty listed the marriages on that date "to the best of … [his] recollection" since his previous report. In 1840, with his father Thomas having married and moved to Mecklenburg County, Major was the head of his household in Lunenburg County. In 1850 the Prince George County Census showed Major living with a woman named Elizabeth. The Census also called him Major Cumbia. In 1853 Major W. Cumbea for $500 bought the Garrett house and about 100 acres in Dinwiddie County. He sold the property, called 150 acres, for $2,750 in 1856. The 1860 Census indicated that he lived in Prince George with a woman named N.B. (Nancy B. Morgan Cumbia). Major's children with Nancy were named Thomas, John, William, and Mary.

Major married Adelia Mary Hobbs on October 24, 1860. With Adelia, according to the 1870 Census, he had a son named M.J.C. and twin infant sons. The Bureau of Vital Statistics records the birth of twin sons on December 1, 1868. M.J.C. probably should have been recorded as M.J.E., for Major James Edward. Cousin Susan Lloyd reported that James was born on August 6, 1862. One of the twins was evidently James' brother, Willard Glover. The Prince George County Birth Register and the Bureau of Vital Statistics record that Major and Adelia had a daughter named Harriett (as in Harriett Early Wells), born on July 25, 1871. According to information provided by Cousin Steve Cumbea, that is the birth date on Willard's tombstone. I do not know how to explain this discrepancy, but a guess is that Willard, whose parents died when he was a toddler, may have been mistaken about his birth date. It seems more likely that the birth record is wrong and that the twins were fraternal, with one of them being the daughter named Harriett. There is a death record of a Harriett Cumbea, who died in Richmond in 1873.

A child named David Cumbia died in 1864, and he was buried near Nancy in Blandford Cemetery in Petersburg, Virginia. Major was probably the father of David, but the cemetery records do not indicate the names of the parents. Major's son named William is also buried at Blandford, near Nancy. A veteran of the War Between the States, unmarried, he died from tuberculosis at 27 in 1869. The death record identified his mother as Nancy B. Cumbia. The father's name was left blank, possibly a sign of continuing hostility after a divorce. (There is some uncertainty over the ending of Major and Nancy's marriage, for Major was identified as a widower when he married Adelia, but Nancy's death was recorded as occurring a year later.) William was the William A. Cumbia from Lunenburg County, whose Civil War service record I had found while doing research for the family reunion in 2000.

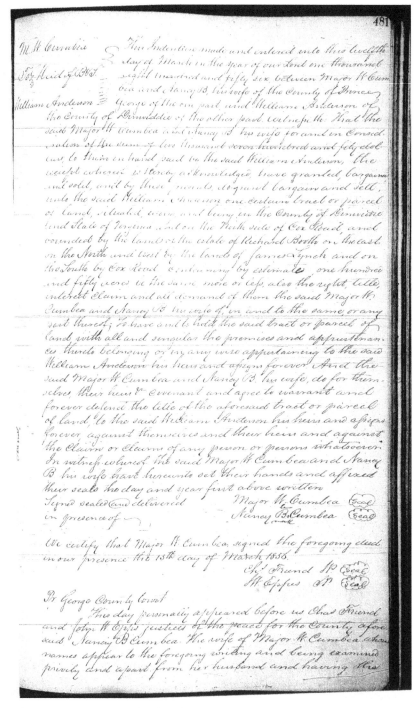

Figure 2.6 Record of sale of the Garrett House property

The deaths of Major and Adelia, while their children were very young, partly explain why finding information about the descendants of Major has been difficult. I have had some limited success, thanks to a lot of help from Susan Lloyd, Steve Cumbea, and Larry Mills.

After the death of Adelia in 1873, Wesley Friend, a son of Major's former employer, was Administrator of Major's estate. The sons, Willard Glover and James Edward, were placed in an unidentified orphanage in Richmond. Steve Cumbea reported that later they were raised in a foster home in North Carolina.

Willard Cumbea married Mary Shaw Hatch on January 18, 1898.They had three daughters – Genevieve, Lina Evangeline, and Arlene Virginia - and a son named James Major Weatherford, the father of Steve Cumbea. They also had a son who was stillborn and who was buried in Chicago. Willard's family moved from Virginia to Chicago, Illinois, then to Nebraska, and finally to Missouri in 1910. Willard died on February 25, 1917, in a wagon accident.

Mary worked very hard in a garment factory to support her family. Genevieve moved to Indiana in order to live with her Aunt Myra Hobbs, and she went to high school there. (Myra, in a time when professional women were few, became the first licensed chiropractor in Indiana.) Genevieve died in her sleep at the age of 22, with the cause of her death unknown. Lina married Virgil Degraffenreid. After years of farming, they opened a hotel and restaurant, becoming successful entrepreneurs. Arlene, according to Larry Mills, "was a prototypical 'Rosie the Riveter'. She worked at a Ford plant in Kansas City where they made airplane engines. She was an inspector checking the tolerances of engine parts with gauges." Arlene died on January 24, 2009. Lina died on February 19, 2005. James Major Weatherford Cumbea, Steve's father, was a salesman. One of the joys of doing research on the family tree has been to read, now and then, that James Major, now in his '90s, has enjoyed the findings.

Figure 2.7 Willard and Mary Cumbea and their daughters, Lina and
Evangeline, photo provided by Larry Mills

76

Figure 2.8 Willard Cumbea, standing on the far left, while working on the railroad, photo courtesy of Larry Mills

Figure 2.9 Marriage record of Willard and Mary Cumbea

Figure 2.10 Aunt Myra Hobbs

Mary worked very hard in a garment factory to support her family. Genevieve moved to Indiana in order to live with her Aunt Myra Hobbs, and she went to high school there. (Myra, in a time when professional women were few, became the first licensed chiropractor in Indiana.) Genevieve died in her sleep at the age of 22, with the cause of her death unknown. Lina married Virgil Degraffenreid. After years of farming, they opened a hotel and restaurant, becoming successful entrepreneurs. Arlene, according to Larry Mills, "was a prototypical 'Rosie the Riveter'. She worked at a Ford plant in Kansas City where they made airplane engines. She was an inspector checking the tolerances of engine parts with gauges." Arlene died on January 24, 2009. Lina died on February 19, 2005. James Major Weatherford Cumbea, Steve's father, was a salesman. One of the joys of doing research on the family tree was to read, now and then, that James Major ("Bunt"), then in his '90s, enjoyed the findings. Grace died in 2010; James died in 2011.

Figure 2.11 James Major Weatherford and Grace Holman Cumbea, parents of Steve Cumbea, photo provided by Steve Cumbea

Willard's brother, James Edward Cumbea, Jim, married Lula Harville in 1886, and they lived in Georgia. He died on May 20, 1949. Jim and Lula had two children, Mabel Lanier and Willard Earl (called Buddy). Buddy never married. Mabel had six children. She married Olin Mason, Sr., and they had one child who died, then twins who died. She also had daughters named Mabel and Oline. Her son, Olin Mason Stanton, Jr. is Susan Lloyd's father. Susan generously provided the names and dates for Jim's descendants. Although mentioning near contemporaries is not in the scope of this summary, I cannot pass this part of our kinfolk without mentioning that Susan's son, Charles Scott Walker, died in the service of his country in Saudi Arabia in 1991.

Figure 2.12 Steve, Grace, and James Major Cumbea

Figure 2.13 Larry Mills, great- grandson of Major Cumbea, wife Anita, and their children, Maria, Bobbie Jo, Corey, and Tracy

Figure 2.14 James Edward Cumbea, photo provided by Susan Lloyd.

Figure 2.15 Mary Cumbea, Arlene, Lina, and James Major,

Photo courtesy of Steve Cumbea

Trying to learn about the children of Major's marriage to Nancy Morgan, I found records indicating that a John R. Cumbea lived in Richmond in the late 1800s and early 1900s. It seems likely that he was Major and Nancy's son. He and his wife, Catherine, called Kate, had several children, and some of their descendents possibly are still in the Richmond area. Although I have looked hard for the families of Thomas and Mary, I have not learned any more about them.

Figure 2.16 House at White Hill, the Friend residence, shortly before
it was torn down in the 1930s, courtesy of US Park Service

In December 1845 Major Cumbea took employment as an
overseer. He worked at White Hill, the plantation on which the Battle
of the Crater was fought during the War Between the States. The
owner of White Hill, Charles Friend, kept a very thorough ***Diary***
which now belongs to the Virginia Historical Society.[ix] Mr. Friend's
Diary has provided a detailed look at the operation of White Hill and,
in particular, the activities of "Mr. Cumbea." He managed the labor
of about 65 slaves, growing at first mainly corn and wheat, later also
growing tobacco. Friend mentioned that Mr. Cumbea did the
carpentry work on the plantation. Sometimes Major managed the
farm for long intervals when his employer was absent, and Major
kept the records of his management. Mr. Friend noted that Mr.
Cumbea had done a fine job of record keeping. (Major's mother,
Agnes, signed her own Consent to marry, so perhaps she taught
Major to read and write.) I have tried without success to identify
some records in Major's own hand. I have also tried, so far without
success, to find a photograph of M.W. Cumbea.

Dr. William Scarborough mentioned M.W.Cumbea in his book
The Overseer: Plantation Management in the Old South.[x] He
described Cumbea as a good example of an "able and ambitious

overseer." Dr. Scarborough wrote at length about the social position of overseers in the Old South. (Major's brother, George, and his father, Thomas, also sometimes worked as overseers.) Socially they were distinctly beneath their employers, not permitted to socialize with the owners or their families, and they were also forbidden to socialize with the slaves they supervised. Overseers were seldom allowed to have their own families live with them, nor could they have guests. They were on call for 24 hours a day, usually for a year at time. They could be quickly dismissed if the owner was displeased with their work. Often characterized as brutal task masters, overseers were more likely to be people who understood the people they supervised and who had the ability to persuade. Overseers sometimes were black or of mixed race heritage. (In some Southern states, blacks were also slaveholders.) Being an overseer was a way to accumulate capital, if the overseer had the will to save, but the profession was very hard on the man himself and on his family. Major was paid $150 a year when he began to work for Mr. Friend, and his salary eventually grew to $250 a year. Major had his small dwelling near the Friend family's house, and he had a vegetable garden and the services of a woman to do his laundry.

According to the White Hill *Diary*, Major Cumbea was quite capable of hitting or whipping a slave who did not work well or who had left the plantation without permission. On Major's behalf, it can be said that such was the common practice at the time. (Flogging was a punishment that was applied to white people as well.) Also, the instances when Major whipped slaves seem to have been few. It is possible that he knew enough about the slaves to be able to motivate them with a minimum of physical brutality.

Figure 2.17 Foundation of the Friend house, as it looked in 2004, photo by author

Given that Major Cumbea managed White Hill plantation, a few words about life there and the treatment of the Friend plantation slaves, as remembered by Friend's daughter, Jennie, may be relevant and interesting.

Before the War Between the States, the Friend family's primary residence was in Petersburg. The farm, White Hill, was a comfortable, ideal place to escape city life. After the Civil War, when the family could no longer afford two homes, the farm was a place to earn a living. Moving to the plantation after the War, the family found the residence gutted and the farm almost unrecognizable. An artillery observation post had been built atop the house. The furniture had reportedly been sent north. The woods had been cut down, and the fields were obliterated. People tilling the ground often unearthed dead bodies. The Friend family supported itself in part by collecting the $5 payments that the United States paid for each skeleton with a skull. Friend's daughter, Jane, remembered a toddler relative proudly displaying the human skull she had found out in the fields. Charles Friend lived only a few years after the War, and his daughter blamed the strain of overwork and worry for his early death.

Figure 2.18 Burial site of Charles Friend at Blandford Cemetery

Mr. Friend often included in his notes observations of the health of the servants. If they were ill or pregnant, they were worked "in the house" or not at all. Although slaves would be used to drain wet fields or to shovel snow, they mainly worked inside when the weather was very wet or too cold. Various measures, for instance the cleaning and whitewashing of the dwellings, were undertaken for "the preservation of the health of the Negroes." Religious instruction was provided, including weddings and funerals. Slaves did not work on Sundays or on holy days such as Christmas or Easter.

Male slaves who desired to marry were expected to ask permission from Mr. Friend. Friend would arrange for the pastor to officiate, and the plantation would have the day off for the wedding. The newly married couple would receive its "own" dwelling, where it could live as a family. Although Virginia law did not recognize the slave marriages, Mr. Friend seems to have respected them, and he kept the slave families together. On at least one occasion, a slave was allowed to miss work due to the illness of his wife.

Trusted slaves were often sent into Petersburg to haul manure back to the farm for use as fertilizer. Untrustworthy slaves would be punished by whipping, and if they continued to give evidence of dishonesty, they would be sold. Slaves who ran away sometimes returned to the plantation. A female slave named Molly returned after being AWOL for about five months, and she was pregnant. Friend wrote that she must be whipped, but that the "disagreeable duty" would have to wait until after the birth of her baby. Returning slaves would be whipped and then readmitted to the family. Slaves would sometimes resist being whipped, but with enough force the whippings would be accomplished anyway. Friend, indicating that runaways were one of the effects of living near a town like Petersburg, wrote that "John who was flogged on Saturday took himself off and has not returned - no one of my servants can be corrected by an overseer that does not run off [without running away] -so much for having a town near."

Mr. Friend seemed to think of the plantation as a large family, and he once wrote that chicken pox was going "through the family, black & white." The Friend *Diary* begins with an account of the funeral of Charles' father. An elderly slave testified that the deceased man had been a very kind master, more like a father than a master to the servants of the plantation.

Mr. Friend apparently trusted most of the slaves, and he believed that they accepted their state in life. Friend's daughter wrote that he always, to the end of his life, believed that slavery was a normal condition for certain people, and he believed that experience and the Bible justified his belief. Charles Friend was surprised and disappointed when many of the servants joined the Union troops-and the overseer, a successor of Major Cumbea-in looting White Hill when US troops occupied the area.

After Emancipation, only a few of the elderly slaves chose to stay on the farm. Jennie Friend's memoirs recorded that former slaves occasionally visited White Hill after emancipation. Sometimes the visits seemed motivated by sincere friendship. At other times, the visits seemed to be merely opportunities to gloat over the decline in Charles Friend's fortune.

The Friend *Diary* recorded the day to day operation of the plantation, and Friend frequently mentioned Major, first as Mr. Cumby, then as Mr. Cumbea. He sowed the wheat on the fields of the plantation, built some of the fences and out buildings, spayed the animals, and supervised the labor of the slaves. When Friend introduced the growing of tobacco on the White Hill Plantation, he made use of Major's expertise, mentioning Major's experience as a tobacco grower in his youth.

A carpenter as well as a farmer, Major Weatherford Cumbea was evidently a person with considerable mechanical aptitude. Mr. Friend mentioned that one time the threshing machine broke down, and it worked only after Mr. Cumbea had repaired it.

Mr. Friend, a devout man who arranged religious instruction for the slaves, also noted that on June 28, 1851, during the funeral for the child of a slave named Penda, Mr. Cumbea was absent. Friend added that it was "the hottest day of the year."

Friend wrote in April 1858 that the slaves did not work before breakfast, due to the illness of Mr. Cumbea.

Before the War, in 1858, Major bought his own 58 acre farm. In December of that year, he left the employment of Mr. Friend, whose *Diary* noted that Mr. Cumbea had lived with him for 13 years. Major's farm was in Prince George County, 7 miles northwest of the Courthouse, bordered on one side by the Appomattox River and on another by the corporate limits of Petersburg, across the River and upstream from the present location of South Park Mall. The northeastern part of the farm is now a landfill. According to Major's obituary, which was provided by Steve Cumbea, the homestead was called Palestine. One wonders if Major thought of his farm as his promised land.

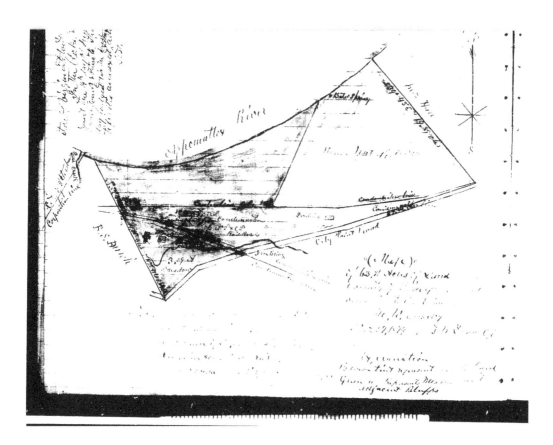

Figure 2.19 Plat of Major Weatherford Cumbea's farm, Prince George County Deed Book 31, p. 240

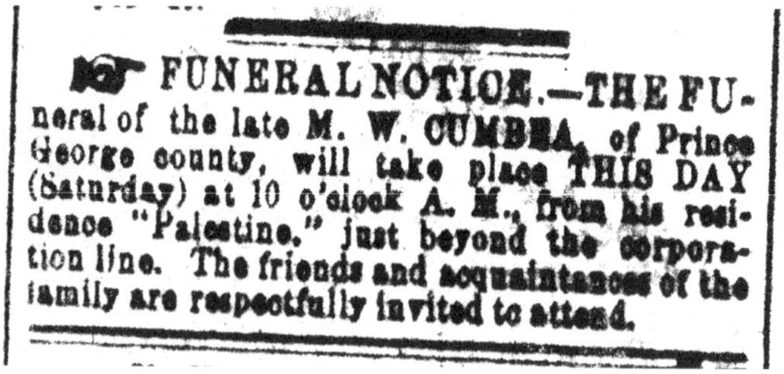

FUNERAL NOTICE.—THE FU-
neral of the late M. W. CUMBEA, of Prince
George county, will take place THIS DAY
(Saturday) at 10 o'clock A. M., from his residence "Palestine," just beyond the corpora-
tion line. The friends and acquaintances of the
family are respectfully invited to attend.

Figure 2.20 Funeral Notice for M.W.Cumbea, from microfilm at
Library of Virginia

Figure 2.21 The site of Major's farm as it looks today

Figure 2.22 Iron Bridge in Petersburg, at the edge of Major Cumbea's farm, in 2006, photo by author

Figure 2.23 Appomattox River, with Major Cumbea's low grounds in the distance

Five slaves lived on Major's farm. I was able to learn the name of only one, a male child named Washington. The slaves were a male, 55, a female, 18, another male, 17, and two young male children. As far as I know, only three Cumbia ancestors, including Major, owned slaves. (Edward Cumby in Halifax County and Major Cumbee in Charlotte County owned slaves.)

In spite of trying, I have not yet been able to learn with certainty what happened to the slaves of Major Cumbea after Emancipation. It seems likely that they had escaped to the Union lines, where they were treated as contraband. There were at least two black Cumbys in Chesterfield County in 1870, a man and a woman, both elderly. There is disagreement among various authorities in regard to slave surnames. I have noted numerous cases in which freed slaves apparently did take their former masters' surnames. (The many black Skipwiths in Mecklenburg County are an example.) I also have read arguments that, contrary to the common assumption, freed slaves were unlikely to take the names of their former masters. If anything, they tended to put social distance between themselves and their former owners, even if they chose out of necessity to stay on the plantations. They were more likely to take the family names of admired figures, such as Abraham Lincoln, Frederick Douglas, or John Brown. One cannot, therefore, deduce with certainty from the names of the black Chesterfield Cumbys that they were former slaves of Major. Perhaps they were. One can guess that if they were former slaves of M.W. Cumbea – which is a big "if"- there might have been some special bond between former master and former slave, something perhaps unusual in the days after the War Between the States.

In about 1870 Major sold to the Southside RailRoad Company a right of way through his farm. (General Mahone, of Civil War fame, was the railroad CEO.) The railroad paid Major $500, more than many families earned in a year in those days. (The expected income from George Cumby's farm was estimated at $50 per year.) When it must have seemed as if all money worries were behind them, Major Weatherford Cumbea contracted meningitis. He died on May 10, 1872, at the age of 55. He left several large medical bills to be settled by his estate, so it seems that the death may not have been sudden. Major's widow, Adelia, took legal steps to protect herself and her children by using the Homestead Act, but she died from unknown causes on November 8, 1873. Her sons were sent to an orphanage in Richmond and then to a foster home in North Carolina. John Cumbea, who was probably one of Major's sons by Nancy Morgan, had the property after Adelia Cumbea's death. There was a long, slow lawsuit of Cumbea vs. Cumbea, in which the children of Major and Adelia sued John Cumbea, through their guardian, Wesley Friend, for their part of the inheritance. When the suit was settled, after all expenses were paid, $54 were left for the support of James Edward and Willard Glover Cumbea. It is possibly significant that there is no record of John's paying taxes on the estate of Major Weatherford Cumbea. He may have foreseen what was coming- the judgment in favor of the brothers- and decided to cut his losses. A John R. Cumbea, possibly Nancy's son, lived in Richmond until 1922.

Major Weatherford Cumbea was, as far as we know, the big achiever of his generation of the Cumby family. (There were at least three other brothers, and we do not know anything about their achievements.) Major, in spite of the illiteracy of his father, learned to read and write. He worked hard and accumulated capital. He owned his own farms, first in Dinwiddie, then near Petersburg, and he was one of the few family members who had slaves. Major was paid by the railroad in order move gravel across his land. When the future must have looked bright, M.W. Cumbea contracted meningitis and died. His wife died about a year later, and the children were sent to an orphanage. His property was sold, and most of the money went to pay off debts. My generation did not even know that Major Weatherford Cumbea had existed. I drove by the site of his farm almost daily, with no awareness that he had lived there. It is ironic that the previously unknown brother left, in the form of the Friend *Diary*, a detailed account of his daily life.

Confederate Service Records

At the Library of Virginia I found a work called ***The Virginia Regimental Histories Series***.[xi] It listed soldiers and identified the Confederate Army units in which each soldier served. The microfilms of the service records, often in the form of notes by historians of the Works Progress Administration, were organized according to unit, rather than by name, so, after I could find the unit in which a person had served, I could find his service record. Several interesting discoveries resulted from consulting the Confederate service records.

I found the records for John Henry Cumbia, which confirmed his recollections as reported by the newspaper on his eightieth birthday. He had been a color bearer, in the front lines of battle after battle. He was wounded. He was at the surrender at Appomattox. He was promoted to Lieutenant. He had been everywhere he said he was when he said he had been there. To have survived so many desperate battles, he must have been very lucky or, as his recollections indicate, very fast on his feet.

There is a record of John's applying for retirement due to his wounds sustained at Cedar Creek. John included a reference that emphasized what a good soldier he had been. The answer to his application for retirement –in very faded and difficult writing- was that such a good soldier should stay in the army and do light duty, while going through appropriate channels to apply for retirement.

Bryon Cook, a descendant of Clarence David Cumbia, found an online book called ***One of Jackson's Foot Cavalry***, by Sgt. John H. Worsham.[xii] The book independently verifies John's account of his tearing up the battle flag and passing out pieces of it to his fellow soldiers.

Willie E. Cumby (also called Cumbie) enlisted in Mecklenburg County and transferred to Co F, 21st Va. Infantry on September 4, 1863. He was listed as missing and wounded in action at the Battle of the Wilderness on May 5, 1864. He died from *vulnus sclopeticum*, gun shot wounds, on either May 24 or May 26 (both dates are documented) in the General Hospital at Staunton. The only Willie Cumby in Mecklenburg County at the start of the Civil War was a son of George and Pamelia Cumby. Robert Allen's older brother named Willie therefore probably did not, as my earlier paper assumed, survive the war. According to the webpage of Thornrose Cemetery in Staunton, the cemetery is the final resting place of 1777 soldiers, with about 700 who were unidentified. Willie probably lies buried with his comrades at Thornrose.

The family Bible of Oscar and Althea Cumbia mistakenly indicates that William Allen Cumbia was Robert Allen's brother. William Allen Cumbia was John Henry Cumbia's grandson.

Sgt. Worsham also reported the death of Willie, called William "D." Cumbia. On page 184, Worsham recorded that Willie had promised to contribute $5 for the support of soldier's widows and orphans. That record and his military service may be the only evidence we will ever have of the character of Willie Cumbia.

The 1850 Census of Mecklenburg County indicated that Willie was born in about 1843, which would mean that he would have been about 21 at his death in 1864. I have carefully checked the marriage records for Mecklenburg, Brunswick, and other Counties to look for a record of a marriage for Willie Cumbia, without finding one.

A white Willie Cumbie, born in Virginia, moved to Texas with his black wife and children after the Civil War. One is tempted to hope that Robert Allen's brother survived the war after being mistakenly listed as killed, but there is so far no evidence to support that hope.

I found the records for James Lewis Cumbea. James, as Dorothy Cumbea indicated, had been an ambulance driver. He was wounded slightly at the Battle of Winchester. When James' widow, Emily, applied for a pension, James' former commanding officer wrote that he had always been a brave soldier.

John and James (and Carolyn Davis's ancestor, W.T. Davis) enlisted on the same day, June 20, 1861. John and Willie were in the same battle when Willie received his fatal wounds.

James Pritchett, a man who was probably Catherine Cumby Pritchett's husband- he was the right age and from Mecklenburg County- died from pneumonia on April 5, 1863, while serving in the Confederate Army. He was buried in a mass grave at Blandford Cemetery in Petersburg, VA. The staff at Blandford informed me that in 1863 so many soldiers and civilians died that it was impossible to individually mark the graves. I looked for some record that Catherine and the children were in the Petersburg area- or anywhere- during the War, but I did not find any. There is no known record of their lives after 1850.

Robert W. Cumby, a son of Peter and the neighbor of Agnes in Campbell County, died at division hospital on July 20, 1864.

Edward Green Cumby (later called Cumba), the son of Thomas and Martha Cumby, George Cumbia's half brother, enlisted on May 18, 1861, in Boydton, VA. He was a private in the 38th Inf. Co G. Twice he was listed as deserted, but he returned to service and was taken prisoner at Amelia Court House on April 5, 1865. He was sent to City Point (now Hopewell), then to Point Lookout, Maryland, where he was released on June 10, 1865. His records describe him as having a dark complexion, brown hair, grey eyes, and being five feet and eight and a quarter inches tall.

Interestingly, for the researchers of the family, Thomas Cumby, Jr., was killed at the Battle of Sharpsburg on September 17, 1862. His back pay was sent to his father at Evergreen P.O., VA. I have not been able to establish with certainty a connection between "our" Thomas and the above Jr., but it seems possible that George, Major, and Catherine had a sibling named after their father and that he was killed in the War Between the States.

William A. Cumbia, a son of Nancy B. and Major W. Cumbia,

enlisted in Richmond in the Virginia Heavy Artillery on March 17, 1862. He was marked AWOL on June 27, 1862. He was present in the Confederate Army from December 31, 1862 until August 31, 1864. He was detailed to the Commissary Department on October 31, 1864. William was taken prisoner at Burkeville, Virginia, on April 6, 1865, taken to Point Lookout, Maryland, and released on June 2.

Paschal Y. Cabiness, Ann Eliza Cumby's husband, served as a Private in the VA 34th Infantry Co. B. He was detailed as a cook in 1864. His commanding officer wrote that he was a "deserving and faithful soldier." Paschal applied for a pension in 1908, when he was 72 years old. He wrote that he had been a carpenter. He stated that he served in the Confederate Army for three years. He described his disability as "deafness, bodily infirmities and old age." He stated that he was at the surrender in 1865.

Alexander Griffith, Mary (Mrs. Robert Allen) Cumbia's father, enlisted at Boydton on July 25, 1861, expecting to serve for one year. He was called a teamster and a wagon driver. He was sick at home in January, 1862, and he was at Chimborazo Hospital No. 1 on August 2, 1862. He was captured on July 5, 1863, near Williamsport, Maryland. He was admitted to the USA General Hospital at Chester, Pennsylvania, on July 14, 1863; then he was transferred to City Point, Virginia on September 17, 1863. Present at Yorktown on April 1, 1864, he was absent in May and June because he was "detailed to procure fresh horse." He said he was at Appomattox Court House at the surrender.

Mecklenburg County Chancery Court Records

Cindy Huggett also found that the Library of Virginia Archives Section stores the Chancery Court documents of Mecklenburg County. She pointed out that several of those cases pertained to the Cumby family. I was able to find the cases, study them, and learn more about the family history.

One of the most interesting cases was Drumwright & Executor vs. Cumby. About 50 pages of documents related to this case are in the Archives of the Library of Virginia. This case involved the debts owed by George Cumby, secured by the family farm. As early as 1857, the family was in serious economic trouble. In 1860 George placed his X on a deed of trust that listed his property as about a hundred acres, one sorrel horse, four cows and calves, five hogs, and five sheep, as well as tools and furniture. To prevent foreclosure, Col. Charles S. Hutcheson- a wealthy landowner, lawyer, judge, and politician - paid the debt, and George Cumby owed the money to Col. Hutcheson. There were more charges, more lenders, and more interest, and the total debt increased over the years. In 1875 the farm was sold at Jubilee Auction by the order of the court. A very interesting part of the court record is the deposition of George Cumby. (Reading the deposition is almost like hearing George talk across a century and a quarter of time.) He stated that he thought he had paid off most of the debt by working as an overseer for a Mrs. Love. He also said he had been paid in Confederate money, which had become worthless. In another lawsuit involving Col. Hutcheson, George testified that he had tried to pay off Hutcheson with Confederate money, and he stated that the Colonel had refused to accept the money as payment.

Wondering where George's family lived after the loss of the farm, I checked the 1880 census and found that Robert Allen lived with his father and stepmother in the Flat Creek District of Mecklenburg County. There were no other individuals living in the home. Evidently George and Lucy did not have any children. One wonders if George hoped to match his father's feat of re-marrying and starting a new family in his old age. Perhaps Lucy was unable to have children, for the cause of her death was identified as "womb." When Robert Allen identified the relationship upon her death, he identified himself as her (step) son.

I noticed with some surprise that neighbors included John and Mary Garnes, with a son named Adolphus. Years later, when Robert bought the Cumbia farm in Brodnax, Adolphus bought a farm north of and adjacent to the home place.

Another interesting case was the case of Sallie Cumby vs. Green Cumby. (Sallie was Lucy Tucker's sister.) Sallie sued Green for divorce, alleging that he had committed adultery with a neighbor called Dinks Crowder. (In the colorful language of the day, Sallie's lawyer referred to Dinks Crowder as "one lewd prostitute.") Sallie alleged that she received no support from Green, and she could not obtain employment as long as she was a married woman. Several neighbors, including George Cumby, gave depositions. One can imagine George squirming as he gave his testimony, trying to tell the truth while knowing that he was testifying against his half brother. George Morgan, the husband of Green's sister, Lucy Ann, also testified against Green. George testified that Green "stays at her house and has his washing done at her house." Sallie won her suit and was granted a divorce. Green married Miss Margaret "Dinks" Crowder in 1880. Willie Munn has written an interesting history of this branch of the Cumba family.

An interesting development from studying the family tree is that we have met first in cyberspace and now face to face a descendant of Green and Dinks Cumba, Willie Munn, who lives in Columbia, SC. Willie transcribed the proceedings of the divorce of Sallie and Green. He pointed out that Green and Margaret had children named Thomas and Martha Roberta, "Patsy." He notified me later that Green and Margaret also had a daughter named Virginia Ann. Willie found and shared wonderful photos of Green, Margaret, and their children, Tom and Pattie Lee, as well as Tom's family.

Martha Roberta Cumba, also called Pattie Lee, was Willie's grandmother.

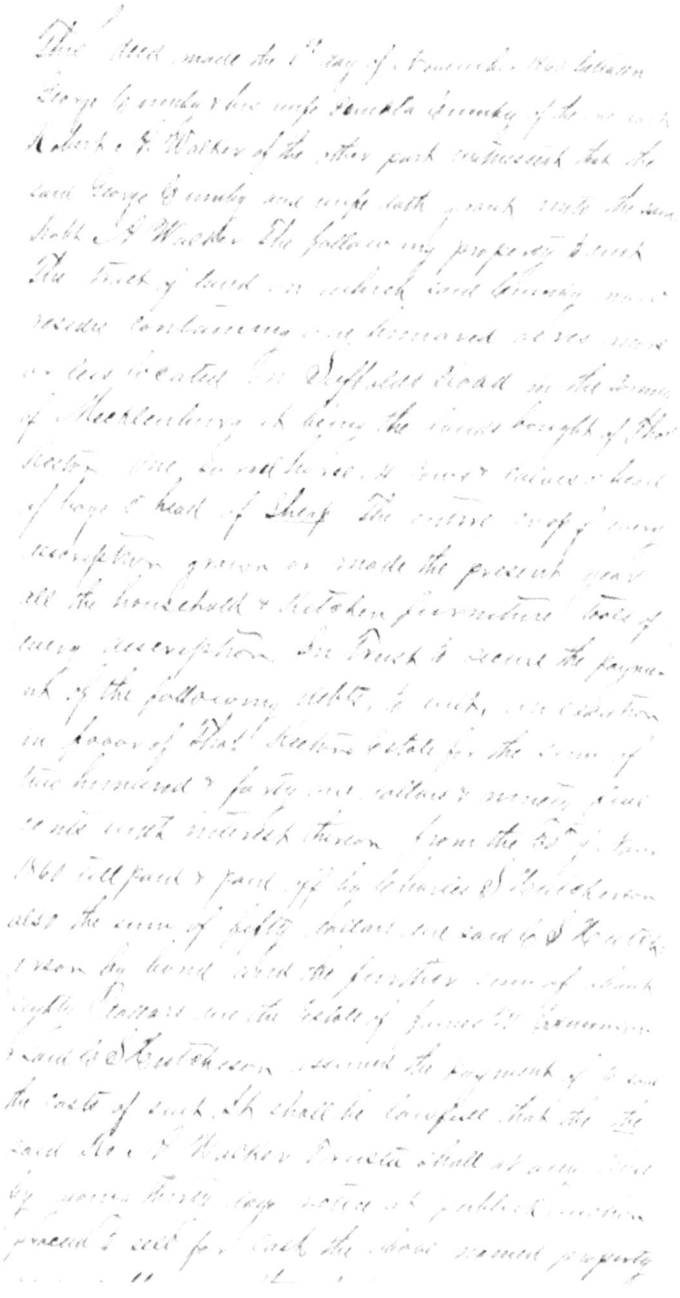

Figure 2.24 Deed of Trust

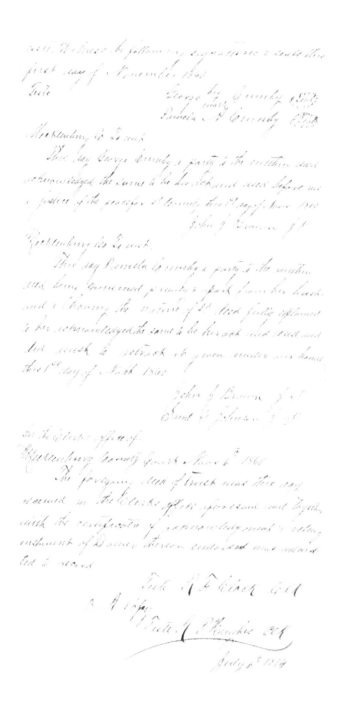

Figure 2.25 Second page of Deed of Trust, with G. Cumby's mark

Figure 2.26 Edward Green Cumba, son of Thomas and Martha
Cumby, half brother of George Cumby, courtesy of Willie Munn

An interesting development from studying the family tree is
that we have met first in cyberspace and now face to face a
descendant of Green and Dinks Cumba, Willie Munn, who lives in
Columbia, SC. Willie transcribed the proceedings of the divorce of
Sallie and Green, and he wrote a history of his branch of the family.

He pointed out that Green and Margaret had children named Thomas and Martha Roberta, "Patsy." He notified me later that Green and Margaret also had a daughter named Virginia Ann. Willie found and shared wonderful photos of Green, Margaret, and their children, Tom and Pattie Lee, as well as Tom's family. Martha Roberta Cumba, also called Pattie Lee, was Willie's grandmother.

Figure 2.27 Margaret Crowder Cumba, her son, Tom, and his wife, Annie Parker, son Raeford, and daughter, Alma, photo provided by Willie Munn.

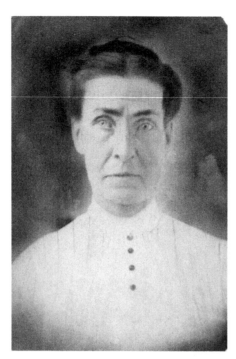

Figure 2.28 Margaret "Dinks" Crowder Cumba, courtesy of Willie
Munn

Figure 2.29 Margaret Cumba and her granddaughter, Margaret
Moseley, photo courtesy of Willie Munn

Figure 2.30 Margaret Moseley, photo courtesy of Willie Munn

Figure 2.31 Lucy Ann Moseley, granddaughter of Green and
Margaret Cumba, daughter of Virginia Cumba Moseley, photo
provided by Willie Munn

Willie informed us that Green, a night watchman, died on April 27, 1919, and that Green and Margaret are buried in the Sunset Hills Cemetery in Littleton, North Carolina. Green's son named Thomas is also buried there.   Willie has continued to be a friendly and interested "new" member of the Cumbia family, often providing photographs and genealogical data.

Figure 2.32 Cumbia cousins, Willie Munn and Sam Whitby

Figure 2.33 Pattie Lee Cumba, Willie Munn's grandmother, photo provided by Willie Munn

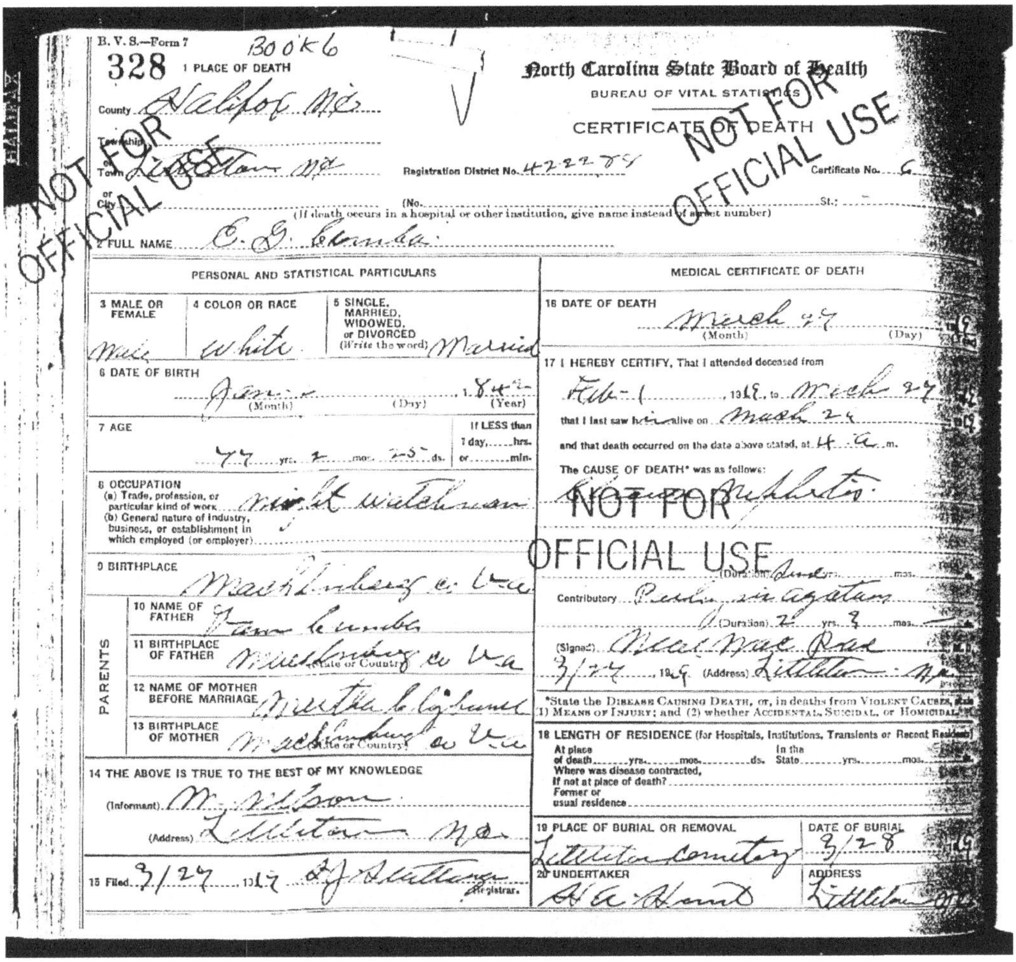
B. V. S.—Form 7 Book 6

328 1 PLACE OF DEATH

North Carolina State Board of Health

BUREAU OF VITAL STATISTICS

CERTIFICATE OF DEATH

NOT FOR OFFICIAL USE

County Halifax NC

Township

Town Littleton NC Registration District No. Certificate No. 6

or City (No. St.; (If death occurs in a hospital or other institution, give name instead of street number)

2 FULL NAME E. G. Cumba

PERSONAL AND STATISTICAL PARTICULARS

3 MALE OR FEMALE Male | 4 COLOR OR RACE White | 5 SINGLE, MARRIED, WIDOWED, or DIVORCED (Write the word) Married

6 DATE OF BIRTH Jan (Month) (Day) 184[illegible] (Year)

7 AGE 77 yrs. 2 mos. 25 ds. If LESS than 1 day, hrs. or min.

8 OCCUPATION (a) Trade, profession, or particular kind of work Night watchman (b) General nature of industry, business, or establishment in which employed (or employer)

9 BIRTHPLACE Mecklenburg Co Va

PARENTS

10 NAME OF FATHER Tom Cumba

11 BIRTHPLACE OF FATHER (State or Country) Mecklenburg Co Va

12 NAME OF MOTHER BEFORE MARRIAGE

13 BIRTHPLACE OF MOTHER (State or Country) Mecklenburg Co Va

14 THE ABOVE IS TRUE TO THE BEST OF MY KNOWLEDGE

(Informant) M. Wilson

(Address) Littleton NC

15 Filed 3/27 1919 Registrar.

MEDICAL CERTIFICATE OF DEATH

16 DATE OF DEATH March 27 (Month) (Day) 19[illegible]

17 I HEREBY CERTIFY, That I attended deceased from Feb 1 1919, to March 27

that I last saw him alive on March 2[illegible]

and that death occurred on the date above stated, at 4 a.m.

The CAUSE OF DEATH* was as follows:

NOT FOR OFFICIAL USE

(Duration) mos.

Contributory

(Duration) 2 yrs. 3 mos.

(Signed)

3/27 1919 (Address) Littleton NC

*State the DISEASE CAUSING DEATH, or, in deaths from VIOLENT CAUSES, state (1) MEANS OF INJURY; and (2) whether ACCIDENTAL, SUICIDAL, or HOMICIDAL.

18 LENGTH OF RESIDENCE (for Hospitals, Institutions, Transients or Recent Residents) At place of death yrs. mos. ds. In the State yrs. mos. Where was disease contracted, if not at place of death? Former or usual residence

19 PLACE OF BURIAL OR REMOVAL Littleton Cemetery | DATE OF BURIAL 3/28 19

20 UNDERTAKER | ADDRESS Littleton NC

Figure 2.34 Death Certificate of Edward Green Cumba, Courtesy of Willie Munn

I tried to make the link between the various county branches of the family by extensively studying Campbell, Mecklenburg, Charlotte, and Halifax records.

One of the most interesting findings is that there was an Agnes Cumby living in Campbell County in the early to mid 1800s. She seems to have been too young to have been the wife of Thomas, but she could possibly have been his daughter. The data would indicate that she was born about a year before the date of Thomas and Agnes's marriage. Perhaps she was named after Agnes Weatherford. None of the documents indicate her relationship to Thomas. A woman named Jemima Cumby lived with her, and she was about 16 years younger than Agnes. A child named Virginia Cumby also lived with her. On one census, Agnes gave her occupation as "farmer and wife," but there was no husband in the home in any of the censuses. In 1860 Agnes lived beside Peter Cumby, who at the time of the census was 100 years old and "a day laborer." Robert W. and Peter Cumby lived with their father, Peter. With some difficulty, I found an 1850 Census of Campbell County that showed Agnes and Jemima living with Peter, so evidently Agnes was a daughter of Peter and Nancy Cumby. The ages given for Jemima in the various Censuses do not agree. The 1880 Census identified Jemima as a sister of Agnes. Given the great age of Peter, 85 in 1850, and the difference of 16 years in the ages of Agnes and Jemima, I suspect that Jemima was really Agnes's daughter. Jemima gave the information for Agnes's death record, and she vaguely and somewhat oddly identified herself only as a "relative."

In the early 1800s there were several Cumby and Cumbee families living in Charlotte County. Someone named Major Cumbee, not the same person as Major Weatherford, filed several lawsuits that are recorded at the LVA. There is also a record of his buying two slaves, a mother named Hannah and her daughter Harriot. (In Halifax County Edward Cumby also owned slaves.) There was also a mention of a Thomas Cumbee who had a wife named Susanna. Thomas bought property from William Sublett, the maternal grandfather of Agnes Weatherford, selling the property later at a big profit. Given that Major Weatherford Cumbea was born in Charlotte County, these data were very interesting. I wondered about the relationship between Major Cumbee and George Cumby's father, thinking perhaps that they were brothers. I finally found documents which showed that the older Major was a son of Thomas and Susanna Cumbee. There is a document that identifies the elder Thomas as Thomas Senior, so "our" Thomas was probably the older man's son. The older Major likely was, therefore, an uncle of George Cumby and Major Weatherford Cumbea. Susanna probably was their grandmother. Thomas and Susannah sold their property and moved to Campbell County, possibly to be near Peter and Emmanuel. Thomas died in Campbell County in 1817.

The largest known concentration of Cumby, Cumbo, and Cumbie individuals in the mid 1800s lived in Halifax County. I have not been able to exhaustively establish the connections, but Thomas Cumby lived in Halifax County when he married Agnes Weatherford. In the late 1700s there were two heads of households in Halifax County: Charles and Thomas, Sr. A researcher may then fairly guess that our ancestry passes through one of them. Another researcher, who I will mention later in a supplement to this summary, has done research that indicates the possible family tree that branches through Halifax.

Charles Cumbo married Elizabeth Masciel (also spelled Maskill) in 1786, and his Will includes a list of children named Molly, Sally, Elizabeth, Annis, Nancy, Elexander, William, Charles, and Lucy C. Another Charles Cumbo, evidently the son of the older Charles, married Nancy Cornwall in 1816. By not listing a Thomas among his children Charles indirectly reinforced my guess that Thomas was a son of Thomas Cumbo. The senior Thomas's wife was named Susanna. I have not yet been able to learn her maiden name. There is an obscure deed reference to a female witness named Middleton/Cumbe, and perhaps this refers to Susannah Middleton. To add to the mystery, Peter Cumbo married Dolly Gray in 1806. In Campbell County, Peter Cumby married Nancy Farthing in 1799. According to the Census, Peter and Nancy were still living and together in 1850, so there were at least two nearly contemporaneous people named Peter Cumbo/Cumby. A researcher could do us a good service by continuing to disentangle the ancestries of Charles and Thomas Cumbo.

Lunenburg County Records

Having found the marriage of Major Cumby to Nancy B. Morgan in Lunenburg County in 1835, I wondered if there might be some other records of Thomas Cumby's having been in Lunenburg at about that time. The Lunenburg County records are extensive, but most of them are handwritten, faded, and very hard to read. Even worse, I could not find an index to guide me to family-related documents. For a long time I believed that the records would not be useful to me. Luckily, I learned that the records had been indexed, and I was able to find several references to Major and Thomas.

In 1828 Thomas Cumby was paid from the estate of Peter Epes for his services as overseer. In 1831, at the sale of the estate of Sterling Fowlkes, Thomas bought a carriage and tobacco. In 1836 Thomas bought land on Muddy Creek and the Meherrin River. Muddy Creek runs into the Meherrin River from the north, upstream from Saffolds Road. (The farm that George Cumby bought in 1838 was on Saffolds Road.) Thomas owned about 200 acres, of which 150 were his for life rights and of which 50 were owned "fee simple"-full title. Thomas was sued by several creditors, and his land was sold in 1843 to pay his debts.

I checked the Censuses for Lunenburg County and found some interesting data.

In 1830 Thomas was listed as head of household. He was between 60 and 55. A female, most probably his wife, was between 50 and 45. There were three males between 20 and 15 (George and two brothers). There was a male between 15 and 10 (Major). There were two children, one male and one female (Catherine) five or under. That means that there were six children, three more sons than we knew about. I have tried to identify the three sons, but I have not been successful. It is likely that they are among the Cumbys who lived in Halifax County in the mid 1800s, but I have not yet been able to identify the parentage of the Halifax Cumbys.

Some Cumbys moved from Virginia to Texas before the Civil War, and one of the Texan Cumbys was named Robert. Maybe later it will be possible to identify the parents of that Robert Cumby, in order to say for sure whether or not he was one of the "lost" sons of Thomas and Agnes.

In 1840 Major was listed as head of household. He and his wife were between 30 and 25, and they had four children five or under.

The information gathered so far indicates that Thomas married in Halifax County. He then was in Campbell County, where George was born. Later, he lived, as shown on the 1810 Census, in Charlotte County, where Major was born. Still later, he lived in Lunenburg County. After the death of Agnes, Thomas moved to Mecklenburg County. He married Martha Curtis Tucker, the mother of Green, Lucy Ann, Louisa, and Virginia, and he lived near his son, George.

In 1851 Thomas Cumby, living in Halifax County, according to Mecklenburg Deed Book 33, relinquished "the entire legacy that may be coming to" Martha "from her father[']s estate," "except the interest I may have in the land she now lives on." Martha still lived in Mecklenburg County, Virginia. It seems that Thomas and Martha were, in modern terminology, "separated." Hoping to find a record that would identify once and for all Thomas's parents, I carefully checked the death records for Halifax County and several other counties, but I did not find a record of Thomas's passing.

The Family of Thomas and Susannah Cumbo

In 1782 and 1785 Thomas Cumbo, according to tax records, lived in Halifax County, Virginia. In 1785 his family composed "13 white souls." Because a document calls Thomas Cumbo "Senior" and because our ancestor named Thomas married in Halifax County, I believe that the senior Thomas was probably "our" Thomas's father. Several documents indicate that the wife of the older Thomas was Susannah, so she was a maternal ancestor.

A complication to the above line of reasoning is the presence of the family of Charles Cumbo in Halifax County in the same era. In 1782 Charles' household was "7 white souls." I think it is likely that Thomas and Charles were brothers, and for some time I wondered whether "our" Thomas was a son of Thomas or Charles.

I have tried to establish the identities of the eleven other family members in the Thomas Cumbo household. Using marriage records, one can identify daughters named Molly, Patsy, Margaret, and Rebekkah. Molly married James Mathews in 1790. Patsy married Elisha Smith in 1806. Margaret married John Powell in 1808. Rebekkah married William Trent in 1821. Other possible but as yet unproved siblings are Patience, who married Robert Wilson in 1787, Mary, who married Evan Young in 1792, and Sarah, who married Ezekiel Mathews in 1793. Sons of Thomas and Susannah were Major, who married Margaret Mical in 1804 and Daniel. Possible brothers include Peter, who married Milly Ramsey in 1785, Emmanuel, who married Nancy Farthing, and Charles, who married Nancy Leeson in 1806. Our forebear, Thomas, married Agnes Weatherford in 1804.

Another document, a deed of gift, indicates that John Cumbo, Sr., gave property to Thomas Cumbo, evidently Senior, in exchange for a promise to care for him the rest of his life. The deed of gift indicates that John, Sr., was likely to have been Thomas's father. I have not yet learned the name of Thomas's mother.

Thomas, Sr., sold his property and moved to Campbell County, evidently to be near his sons, Peter and Emmanuel. Thomas died there in 1817. (See *Notes on the Cumbia Family Tree*, to be published in 2011, for an inventory of Thomas's property.) I am continuing to do research in the hope of extending our knowledge of our family tree and history.

Part 3

Ancestry before 1800

Some thoughts on Methodology

Having traced our Cumbia ancestry back to Thomas Cumby in Halifax County, Virginia, in the late 1700s, I wanted to learn about our earlier ancestors, who they were and where they came from. The results of the research will probably surprise you.

When beginning to study the Cumbia family tree, I realized that all the findings might not please potential readers. I had no desire to stir up trouble – to cause hard feelings – to no good end, but I wanted to establish the family genealogy and history as accurately as possible. The decision was made, therefore, to try to establish each relationship with as many official documents as possible. I did this initially with the intention of over-riding doubts and preconceptions. After finding some records that contradicted or seemed to contradict each other, I sought to document with more than one source, in order to decide between different documents.

Also, in the back of my mind, there was always the memory of one relative or another saying, "Well, I always heard that…." Relatives who I loved and respected had their deeply- held beliefs and expectations, and I was reluctant to unnecessarily surprise or disappoint them. The recollections of older relatives were, in themselves, valuable evidence. If contradicting a long-held belief became necessary, I wanted to be able to say why doing so had been necessary.

There was also the testimony of those who had done a little superficial research. I wanted, for example, to be able to answer those who had looked up the family name in a book somewhere. Instead of repeating generalities that might have no relevance to the actual history of the family, I wanted to learn something real about actual relatives and their history. I wanted to be able to answer those who held old and cherished beliefs, such as that the family was part American Indian or Scottish in origin, to be able to say why a belief was correct or incorrect.

Virginia kept fairly complete vital records from 1853 through 1896. In a misguided gesture of fiscal conservatism, Virginia did not keep vital records from 1896 to 1912. The absence of records for the interval of 1896 to 1912 makes it very hard to establish some dates and relationships. (For example, Ann Eliza Cumby Cabaniss probably died during that interval, and the lack of a death record makes it difficult to determine when she died and where she is buried.) Ancestry from 1853 can usually be established with little doubt.

Family trees before 1853 require different methods. Certain records such as marriage records, tax lists, church records, and deeds do still exist, but they often do not explicitly reveal family relationships. Some records were lost due to accidents, fires, or the Civil War. Birth records and death records before 1853 are rare. If someone wants to study a family before 1853, different research methods must be applied. One must collect data other than the usual vital records, then back away and look at the big picture, rather like looking at a puzzle with many missing pieces. Geography, history, and genetics must be taken into account. One must consider names and similar names, and then one must deduce the family relationships. Meaningful hypotheses can begin to emerge even if particular parts of the data remain obscure. I want, here, to begin to present data in such a way that meaningful hypotheses can emerge. Different people may see different figures at the end, but the pictures will at least be recognizable as reasonable conjectures or assumptions.

A few words about the limitations of genealogical methods may be in order here. Family trees assembled by deduction, rather than by using explicitly vital records, are likely to be very incomplete. Early deeds, for example, tend to reveal hints about only the buyers and/or sellers of property. In a time before modern birth control methods and in an agricultural economy, families tended to be large. It could be very possible for a large family to leave either no records or records only for the members who bought or sold property. People who did not marry or who married in another state might not be evidenced. Also, in old marriage records, female surnames are often omitted. Females, much less likely to be landowners, would be underrepresented. Offspring who died as minors would not be counted either. Individuals who moved out of state before purchasing property or marrying would leave little if any trace. In a time of the conquest of the frontier and westward expansion, movement out of state probably occurred often, leading to failure to count all persons. In spite of the limitations, the deductive methods used in genealogy can provide part of the truth and many interesting guesses, making them worthwhile.

In order to make my conclusions more intelligible, I have chosen to change the order of presentation from what it was in earlier sections of this paper. (I also hope to avoid alienating potential readers before they have had a chance to hear me out.) Although in the earlier accounts of the research findings I proceeded from more recent to less recent, I will reverse the order and start the story in the distant past. I will present the facts and state hypotheses to explain the facts. A particular hypothesis concerns the origin in the Cumbia family tree of an unusual genetic trait. Please be patient and bear with me, trying to let a figure emerge from the seemingly unconnected data.

The Historical Data

In the early days of Jamestown, Virginia, there were several people with names like Cumby. For example, a ship captain named Thomas Cumbe brought people to the new world. An early resident of Jamestown was Nicholas Camme (called a gentleman), sometimes transcribed as Combe. The Cumbes at Jamestown were perhaps sons of landed English people who wanted to extend their holdings to the Americas. (Josiah H. Combs found that William Shakespear's neighbors in England were land owners named Combe.) Researchers of the Combs family have collected data on the Jamestown Cumbes and some possible English antecedents. I would encourage readers to look up the Combs family Internet page and study these data for themselves.[xiii] For reasons that will become apparent later, I doubt any direct connection to the similarly named individuals at Jamestown.

I found a record of the transport of a person called a Negro, probably a slave, named Cumby. There were also indentured servants with names like Cumby. Ann Combey, for example, came to Virginia as an indentured servant in 1635. There were probably others, perhaps many others, without existing records. Again, for reasons that I hope to establish, I believe that Cumbias are descendants of one of these indentured servants.

In 1667 Emanuell Cumboo received a land patent for about 50 acres in James City County, Virginia. For reasons that will become apparent, I believe that Emanuell was one of the earliest-perhaps *the* earliest- identifiable ancestor of our line of Cumbias.

Sarah Cumbo was taxed on 53 acres of land in James City County from 1800 to 1812. These 53 acres were probably the land handed down from Emanuell. The ownership by Sarah Cumbo indicates that the name Cumboo sometimes came to be spelled Cumbo.

Also in James City County was William Farthing. Peter and Emmanuel Cumby married daughters of William Farthing in Campbell County in 1799 and 1800, respectively.

Emmanuel Cumbee in 1730 bought from William McBee 200 acres of land in King George County. There is also a record of his having been sued, along with several other men. The suit was later dropped. This Emmanuel is probably not the same as the one mentioned above. He may have been that person's son.

Richard Comboo, who probably was a son of the earlier Emanuel, sold 100 acres in Charles City County in 1724. The land later became part of the plantation of Benjamin Harrison. Richard and his wife Ann had a daughter named Elizabeth, who possibly was an owner of the 53 acres in James City County, mentioned above.

John Cumbo, Sr., likely a son of Richard, was granted a land patent for 150 acres in Surry County in 1724. As historian Paul Heinegg wrote, citing here with permission from Mr Heinegg, "He was in Brunswick County, Virginia in 1738 [Orders 1732-41, 192], and on 2 July 1746 when a deed mentioned land on Peahill Creek and John Cumbo (on the Brunswick County, Virginia line) [DB 1:260]. John was sued by Nathan Edwards on February 5, 1747 in Brunswick County. A Granville County, NC, will mentions a plantation or estate called Cumboes in 1759. John was sued by James Gowen in 1757 in Brunswick County, VA. In 1760 John Cumbo sold 238 acres to Peter Avent. The land was in Maherrin Parish in Brunswick County.The Northhampton Deed Book 3, p. 197, 1764, mentions a deed of gift from John to Thomas Cumbo for "maintaining him in his lifetime." This deed of gift indicates that Thomas was likely to have been John's son.

Other Cumbos in Brunswick County in the mid 1700s include Daniel, Gideon, and Thomas. This Thomas may be Thomas, Sr., who lived later in Halifax County.

In 1767 the *Virginia Gazette* published an advertisement for a runaway slave from Charles City, who was described as "a well made mulatto fellow named *Daniel*, about 5 feet 5 or 6 inches high. He has a forged pass, and passes for a freeman, by the name of *Daniel Cumbo*." [xiv]

The 1810 Census of James City County listed a Daniel Cumbo. Daniel's household consisted of one white tithable (person obliged to pay taxes, probably Daniel himself), with three horses.

As indicated earlier, in the late 1700s in Halifax County there were two heads of households with names like Cumbo: Charles and Thomas Cumbo, Sr. In spite of considerable effort, I have been unable to completely answer the question of which Cumbos/Cumbys were descended from Charles and which were descended from Thomas. Charles' Will listed nine children, none of whom were Thomas, reinforcing the hypothesis that "our" Thomas was a son of Thomas, Sr. I think it is very likely that Charles and Thomas (as well as John, Jr.) were brothers, sons of John, Sr. John Cumbo married Polly Jennings in 1794, and his estate was being settled in 1797. Having found no evidence that he had any children or founded a line of descendants, my guess is that he was a son of John, Sr., and that he died young, without any offspring. It is also possible that John lived to a very old age, and his marriage to Polly may have been a twilight marriage, after the main settling of his Earthly affairs.

A few things can be said about the life styles of these early ancestors. Most of them were farmers, or at least most of them were owners of farms. Few, seemingly only three in the entire Cumbo/Cumbia line, were slave owners. (They were Edward Cumby, Major Cumbee, and Major Weatherford Cumbea. Several ancestors worked as overseers on plantations.)They paid taxes, and some of them contributed to their communities by building and maintaining roads. They often had large families. They often lived to be quite old. Longevity seems to have been a family characteristic.

A Distinctive Genetic Trait in the Cumbia Family

The story of Charles and Thomas Cumbo brings us to a connection with the previous research, which indicated that our direct ancestor, Thomas Cumby, was the father of George and grandfather of Robert Allen.

Some other bits of data bear mentioning and may be hard for some people to accept. At about the time that I started doing research on the family tree, I learned that my youngest son carried the sickle cell trait. Two Cumbia cousins approached me and told me that they were sickle cell trait carriers, indicating that my son received the sickle cell trait through me, through the Cumbia side of my ancestry. Another relative, not a Cumbia but related through Thomas Cumby, has also learned that he carries the trait. Although the sickle cell trait is found in people with North African and Mediterranean ancestry, it is usually associated with black ancestry. In the land patent to Emanuell Cumboo, Emanuell is identified as a "Negro." In 1758, in Charles City County, Richard Combo was hauled into court for not declaring his wife as a titheable (taxable) for being the wife of a free Negro. John, Sr., is identified as a Mulatto. Paul Heinegg found that in 1795 Thomas Cumbee was a Mulatto taxable. Peter and Emmanuel were also Mulatto taxables. In the early 1800s Peter, Emmanuel, John, and Thomas passed for white.

Another two Cumbia relatives approached me and asked if I had found out how keloid growths, usually associated with black genetics, had entered their lines of the family.

Carolyn Davis suggested that I contact a researcher named Dr. G. C. Waldrep, III. He suggested that I contact Paul Heinegg. Heinegg wrote *Free African Americans of Virginia, North Carolina, South Carolina, Maryland and Delaware* , in which he reported the findings of his research on mixed-race families.[xv] One of the lines that he studied is the Cumbo family. He traced the Cumbo family from "a mulatto named Manuel" who was "judged no Slave but to serve as other Christian servants do" in 1644 and freed in 1665. Manuel was possibly the same person who was later called Emanuell Cumboo[,] Negro. (The original document is very hard to read. The name could just as easily be transcribed Combew, Cumbew, or Cumboo.) Emanuel received a patent (a grant) of about fifty acres of land in 1667. Given the small number of people with European names living in the area, given the similarity of the names, and assuming also the small number of freed blacks in the area, I think the likelihood that Manuel and Emanuell are one and the same is good. I would like to present the hypothesis that the earliest known Cumbia ancestor, a source of the Cumbia name, was a black man.

Figure 3.1 Part of the land patent to Emanuell Cumboo Negro, from microfilm at the Library of Virginia

In *James City County: Keystone of the Commonwealth*, historian Martha McCartney pointed out that slaves sometimes converted to Christianity, apparently with the hope that conversion would lead to freedom, for the Christian authorities seemed reluctant for Christians to own other Christians in perpetual servitude. In 1667 Virginia closed that path by legislating that conversion would not affect a slave's condition of servitude. Manuel, called in 1665 "no Slave" and directed to serve "as other Christian servants do," may have just "squeaked by" and gained his freedom in the nick of time.[xvi]

The specific circumstances for the freeing of Manuel are

unknown. Slaves were freed for varied reasons, including outstanding loyalty, bravery, or service to the master. Whatever the particulars, Manuel must have been seen as a loyal and dutiful servant of his owner, William Whittacre, or he never would have been freed.

Heinegg also traced the Cumbo line through an individual of great interest to Cumbias, Thomas Cumbo, Sr., who lived in Halifax County, Virginia, in the mid 1700s. I think it is likely that either Thomas, Sr., or his probable brother, Charles, was George Cumbia's grandfather.

McCartney also wrote about a community of free blacks in the Jamestown/Williamsburg area. William Lee freed his slaves in his Will, and he tried to establish a "normal" – a free public - school on his Hot Water Plantation. He planned to have the freed slaves educated to the point that they could support themselves. Many of the blacks who were freed stayed in the area in the expectation that training or education would be made available to them there. Cumbos were among the free black families living in the area, which came to be called Centerville. Lee's Will seems to have been frustrated by the inaction of various parties. The College of William and Mary declined to accept the responsibility for the normal school, and no real effort to educate the slaves happened. White people living nearby, fearful of free blacks, especially after the murders by Nat Turner, eventually dispersed the African-American community. I think it is likely that some Cumbo ancestors, light skinned, moved and were accepted as whites, allowing the knowledge of their ancestry to be lost. Others stayed in the area and remained part of mixed-race or black society.

The 1850 Census of James City County lists several individuals named Cumber, all identified as mixed-race or black. Perhaps the Cumbo relatives who did not pass as white remained in the area and had their names spelled as Cumber.

I have checked most of the documents cited by Paul Heinegg, and his citations are accurate. Heinegg's research, due to the nature and scarcity of records in the 16 and 1700s, cannot establish the family tree with the rigor that could be had after the 1850s. Most James City County records were taken to Richmond during the Civil War, for safe keeping .The records burned when the Confederates abandoned their capital in the last days of the War. Still, I think that need to accept that what is surprising is also real.

The questions of how and why the descendants of a black man are white have a likely answer. In the mid 1600s in the Colony of Virginia, women were few and in high demand as wives. Heinegg has argued that, contrary to the assumption that racial mixing is the result of masters having raped slaves, most racial mixing began early in colonial history when indentured servants, likely to be white and female, married or had children with free blacks. One of our ancestors was probably a poor white woman, possibly with a name sounding like Cumbo, who gained her freedom by marrying or having children with a free, mixed-race man. Emanuell may have gained his wife by buying her out of her contract of indenture. If Heinegg's guess is correct, then Manuel the mulatto, possibly already a person with a light complexion, may have taken the name Cumboo, which became Cumbo, Cumby, and Cumbia from his wife. Some of his children with a white woman married white people. As the social climate became less friendly to black people, some mixed race Cumbos moved to North Carolina or elsewhere, searching for more favorable conditions. The mixed-race Cumbos with light complexions, who could pass as white, were glad to be accepted as white. They moved to the frontier, including Halifax County, Virginia. If they knew about their ancestry, they kept the knowledge to themselves for their protection. They did not mention their ancestry even to their children, and knowledge of it was lost.

Granddaddy Cumbia once told me that he had ancestors who were full-blooded Cherokee Indians. It seems that he said he had a great-grandmother who was Indian, but my memory is not certain. I regrettably did not pay much attention at the time, for claiming Indian ancestry is very common and probably a part of local culture rather than actual history. The point of bringing up this recollection now is that there possibly was some faded recollection of the mixed-race status of the family. Maybe Granddaddy had heard of his mixed-race heritage from his ancestors. Various historians have alleged that Indians tended to be called Negroes in official documents. I think it is also likely that blacks might claim to have Indian ancestry.

I realize that an African connection may not be a finding that will be welcomed by everyone. Some may be offended simply because they do not like the idea of black ancestry, even if removed by over three hundred years. (At Emanuell's distance, I have 1,024 or possibly more grandparents who could have contributed to my genetic history.) Even if not offended, one may find the connection unexpected and incredible. If I did not know that one of my children and I carry the sickle cell trait and that at least two Cumbia cousins carry it also, I would not take seriously the thought of having African ancestry. We have been white as far back as anyone knows. We are white. Now we are also aware of some non-white ancestry as well.

Objections

I have tried to think of possible objections to the idea of African ancestry and tried to answer them.

How, one might ask, can there be African ancestry when there are no African traits? Sickle cell trait and the tendency to keloids are African traits, so African traits do exist in our family tree.

How can there be African ancestry without dark skin or curly hair? Ancestors who possibly already had light complexions married white people, and their children married white people. Ancestors chose to mate with Caucasions, making the identification of "whiteness" based upon appearance. Sickle cell is not a visible trait. Silent and invisible, the trait hitched a ride down our history. The traits usually associated with black ancestry have been diluted or replaced by traits usually associated with Caucasions. The sickle cell and keloid traits are surviving relics.

How can there have been African ancestry when nobody knew about it? Our ancestors realized that black people were at a disadvantage due to discrimination, and they kept the racial history of the family a secret. Once the people who knew the history had died, the history was lost. Another way of saying the same thing is that people did not know because people did not tell. After no one knew, no one could tell.

Why are only the Cumbias a racially mixed family? According to Heinegg and others, we are far from being alone. Heinegg also documented the mixed race ancestry of a large number of other families. Another was the Coley family, and Mary Allen Cumbia's mother was a Coley. There were mixed-race people named Griffin, perhaps ancestors of Mary Griffith Cumbia. The Farthings, whose daughters married Peter and Emmanuel Cumby, and who were not in our direct ancestry, were a mixed race family. Other families –many others- had the same reasons our ancestors had to keep the black ancestry a secret.

Some interested parties have claimed that Negro and Mulatto were terms that were applied to American Indians, and they have alleged that documents indicating black ancestry really mean Indian ancestry. They point to an act of the Virginia government in 1705. The act decreed that the offspring of whites and Indians would be called Mulattos. In the cases of John and Thomas Cumbo,Sr., both of whom, along with Peter, were identified as mulattos on lists of taxables, this objection has some merit. (Free blacks and mixed race people had to pay special taxes as undesirables.) Emanuell, however, lived in the 1600s. Also, claiming Indian rather than African heritage does not explain the presence of the sickle cell trait in the blood line. African ancestry does explain it. The simplest, most believable idea is that the family has African and white ancestry, with perhaps some Indian ancestry as well.

A few people may think but not want to say that I am attributing negative cultural traits, associated in unkind prejudices with black ancestry, to the Cumbia family. I can only say that people are individuals. One cannot predict character by appearance, especially by so gross a trait as skin color. I am not saying that Cumbias or Cumbia ancestors acted in any given way; I am saying that some of their ancestors had dark skin-period. Skin color does not indicate behavior or character. Surviving records indicate that many of our ancestors were hard-working and ambitious. Emanuel was an at least nominal Christian.

Have I really proved the connection between Emanuell Cumboo and the Cumbia family? Have I really identified the source of the sickle cell trait? "Proved" is a strong word. Given the destruction of James City County records at the end of the War Between the States, I do not believe it is possible to prove the connection with absolute certainty. I do believe I have given an explanation that is plausible, a connection that is likely. As far as connecting the sickle cell trait with Emanuell, I think that is likely also, but it is not proved. The trait could have entered my line from some other (still probably African) source.

Another serious objection involves not the thesis itself – that some Cumbia ancestors were black- but the idea of making the ancestry known. My mother-in-law grew up in Germany when Hitler was in power. She said that someone who discovered Jewish ancestry and made the knowledge public would have been condemning his family to death. She warned that I may be making my family vulnerable to discrimination. As the South neared the War Between the States, any black ancestry – sometimes said as "even one drop of Negro blood"- meant that a person was legally a black. Blacks lacked the rights that we take for granted today: the right to vote, own property, freely associate, and so forth. I have seen Virginia deeds, as recent as the 1950s, with exclusion clauses. The clauses provided that selling land to anyone of African descent would invalidate the deed, making the property revert to its white owner, with the evident intent to keep neighborhoods white. By documenting any black ancestry at all, in a discriminatory state, I would be effectively subjecting my entire family to the loss of its civil rights. This objection has worried me more than any or all of the others, for I share the normal human desire to protect one's family. My answer is that establishing our kinship with the larger human family will encourage us to make sure that a fascist state never takes power in America. Knowing that we have some tenuous connection to black America may encourage us to

126

treat individuals of every race with kindness and respect.

The Daniel Cumbo who was mentioned above, if, as seems to be the case, he was in our line, was a member of a family that had been free for over a hundred years. He had his freedom papers, and they were legitimate. He may have been "set up" by someone who hoped to sell him or perhaps to own him, by alleging that his race indicated his servitude.

Also, if laws like the Racial Integrity Act of 1924 can classify anyone with any black ancestry-with even one drop of African blood-as a "Negro," would we not be doing well for our own selves, if we could make sure that *all* people would be treated fairly and compassionately?

Why not just leave well enough alone? Why stir up dissension at this late hour, when you can just not mention the mixed-race ancestry? My son, David, responded this way: if your goal is telling the truth, and you do not tell the *whole* truth, then you have not told *the* truth. If you want to provide the truth for your posterity and you do not, then you have deprived them of your knowledge. Your descendants will have to do your work all over again, and they may never learn what we know.

Racial mixing occurred much more often than most people would think. It early was not the issue that it would later become. Consider that in Colonial, i.e., English, Virginia social class was much more important than race. There were two classes of people: nobility and commoners. When John Rolfe married Pocahontas and took her to England, society was scandalized, not because a white man had married an Indian, but because a commoner (Rolfe) had married royalty (Pocahontas).

Another way of analyzing society in colonial Virginia, freeing itself from England, finds that the two classes of people were landed aristocracy and everyone else. In a sense, poor white people were at the bottom of the bottom half of the social scale, and they worked and lived in proximity to blacks, free or enslaved. Slaves at least had wealthy people who had a financial interest in their welfare. As long as their masters had enough to eat, they had food to eat, and they had a dwelling, clothes, and medical care. Poor free whites lead a more precarious existence. Indentured white servants were especially vulnerable, for their masters did not have a large investment in them. Indentured servants could be mistreated, even beaten to death, without legal consequences to their masters. Slaves were expensive, and indentured servants were not. Mistreatment of a slave could cost a master a lot of money. The murder of one healthy adult slave would cost an owner about as much as a typical two hundred acre farm. (If great-great grandfather George Cumby had owned one slave, he could have sold him, and he would have paid off the debt that cost him his farm.) The murder of an indentured servant cost a master little, and it was usually not a punishable offense. Indentured servants, therefore, had great incentive to move out of their status, to become free at almost any cost. Furthermore, Virginia still was partly frontier in the 16 and early 1700s. White people and black people had Indians as common enemies. People on the frontier very well might have preferred to stick together rather than be scalped individually. Having fought and lived together, they may have been more likely to continue to get along and to let the past fade away. People who knew the mixed-race ancestry of their neighbors might have been more willing not to tell. Paul Heinegg's work documents numerous cases of cooperation and friendship between white and black neighbors.

There is the possibility that the sickle cell trait entered our family's genetic history by way of Greece, Italy, or North Africa. Cousin David Cumbia reported a family tradition that the Cumbia name was Italian. Comba seems to be a fairly common Italian name. In France there was a family named Combier. (A Greek, Italian, or Arab would probably have encountered the trait in a black ancestor.) If one chooses, he or she may just deny any black African blood in his or her veins. On the other hand, one may decide simply to accept who he or she is. One even may think of the hitherto unknown ancestors with gratitude, for if they had not been, we would not be.

Most of the people who read these words will be Cumbia

kinfolk, many of whom profess to be Christians. I hope that, here at the end, they will forgive a departure from impartiality. Striving to act and evaluate in light of our basic beliefs, I encourage you to look at this data with the light of a Christian world view. It is humbling to claim the kinship of an ancestor who gained his freedom in part because he was "judged" a Christian servant. To those who are offended, I offer the words of Jesus, who instructed us to love our neighbors as we love ourselves. He gave the Samaritan, a member of a despised and demeaned group of people, as the quintessential example of the loving neighbor. Furthermore, Jesus himself advised that those who would be the greatest among us should be the servants of the rest. Instead of allying one's self with the temporary, human bosses of the current time, one would do better to remember and honor the God who is no respecter of persons, who surely is not impressed by the mere color of a person's skin.

Figure 3.2 Sanford Memorial Congregation in 1952, with the author at front near the center, photo from the Whitby family

In the late fifties and early sixties, my childhood and teen years, I attended Sanford Memorial Baptist Church in Brodnax, VA. There were many good things about Sanford Memorial, and I owe it more than I can ever pay back. There were also problems, including one very big one: race. Some members were worried that black people might try to join the church, and others knew that their consciences would not allow them to forbid membership to anyone who sincerely professed faith in Jesus Christ. Cumbia family members were on both sides of this issue. On at least one major occasion, the attendance at a church business meeting voted overwhelmingly to admit any Christian of any color. My mother recalled that a member of the church introduced a motion to close the church before admitting "colored people." He said that voters would show their friendship or enmity toward him by the way they would vote. My mother pointed out that the church Constitution provided for secret votes on controversial subjects, and she demanded that the vote be secret. Only two people voted to exclude membership to blacks. Some people left the church over this issue. Some who did not leave tried to undercut the various pastors, by criticism and failure to support the church financially. In spite of the difficulties, Sanford Memorial has survived and grown. Moreover, seeing African-American faces in the congregation does now happen. What some dreaded and others feared has become reality: white Christians have married black Christians, and their white, black, and brown families are welcome at Sanford Memorial Baptist Church.

It seems that Sanford Memorial was tested on the issue of race – and passed the test.

I enjoy imagining the surprised faces in the great family reunions on the streets of Heaven. His grace is sufficient.

The family tree was not studied in order to learn or teach a moral lesson. I studied the family history primarily because I loved and missed my grandparents, and I hoped to learn more about them and their ancestors. A lesson, however, is inescapable: be careful when you hate a group, for you may find yourself part of that group.

Part 4

Summary and Afterthoughts

Robert Allen Cumbia, a great-grandfather of my generation, was born in 1857 in Mecklenburg County, Virginia. His parents were George Cumby/Cumbia and Pamelia Ann Wells. Robert was the youngest of at least seven siblings. His nearest sibling in age was a sister, Louisa, who died unmarried in 1873. A brother named John Henry Cumbia served in the Civil War and started a branch of the family in Smokey Ordinary, Virginia. A brother named William was killed in 1864 at the Battle of the Wilderness. James Cumbea also served in the Civil War, and he started a branch of the family that survives in the Richmond/Powhatan areas and elsewhere today. A sister named Mary Susanna married David Brooks. A sister named Ann Eliza married Paschal Cabaniss, and they had numerous children, descendants of whom are still in the counties of Mecklenburg and Lunenburg.

George Cumby's parents were Thomas Cumby and Agnes Weatherford. George had a brother named Major Weatherford Cumbia/Cumbea, and a sister, Catherine, who married James Pritchett. George had at least three brothers, the names of whom are unknown. Major had a farm in Dinwiddie and a career as an overseer at White Hill in Prince George County, and then he had a farm on the edge of Petersburg. After the death of his first wife, Nancy B. Morgan, Major married Adelia Hobbs. George and Thomas also worked as overseers.

Agnes Weatherford's father was Rev. John Weatherford, a Baptist preacher who was jailed in Chesterfield County for preaching as a Baptist in Anglican Virginia.

Thomas married Martha Curtis Tucker, many years younger

than Thomas, after the death of Agnes. Thomas and Martha lived on a farm that was given to Martha by her father in Mecklenburg County, near George's family. Thomas and Martha had children named Edward Green, Lucy Ann, Louisa, and Virginia. Green, after an adulterous relationship, was successfully sued for divorce. George lost the family farm in a lawsuit over unpaid debts. Thomas lost a farm in Lunenburg County in a lawsuit over unpaid debts. Neither George nor Thomas could read or write. Thomas Cumby's parents were probably Thomas and Susanna Cumbo/Cumby. They lived in Charlotte, Halifax, and Campbell Counties. Thomas Cumbo (Senior)'s father seems to have been John Cumbo of Brunswick, Charlotte, and Halifax Counties. His father was Richard Cumboo in Charles City County, and his father was Emanuell Cumboo in James City County.

Some Thoughts on the Cumbia Name

I am often asked about the origin of the Cumbia name. People want to know the correct spelling of the name and its nationality.

It is easy to imagine that there was some primal source of a Cumbia clan, and that he set the final and correct spelling of the family name, which has been preserved by true relatives ever since. The truth seems to be more complex. The spelling of the family name varies with the source. It seems that most of our early ancestors could not read or write. The name evidently was spelled phonetically by various record keepers. In other words, they wrote it the way it sounded to them. The earliest "signature" that I have found –a very personalized X - is that of Charles Cumbo, in the late 1700s. Neither the grandfather nor father of Robert Allen could read or write. In most documentation, their names were spelled Cumby, and evidently they were pronounced that way. Major Weatherford's name was recorded as Cumby when he married Nancy Morgan, and the name was spelled Cumbia in the 1850 Census, Cumbea later. Major could read and write, and evidently he pronounced (or began to pronounce) the name with the three syllables that we use today. Our family tradition is that Aunt Dessie Michael changed the spelling to Cumbia. While I believe that is true, I also think it is possible that Robert Allen may have attended his Uncle Major's funeral in 1872, and the third syllable may have entered Robert Allen's family at that time. When Robert's sister, Louisa, died in 1873, her death was reported as the death of a Cumbia. George Cumbia's estate was settled in 1884 with the name spelled Cumbia.

The nationality of the name is probably English, for our ancestors go back to the environs of Jamestown, which was an English settlement. The name is possibly derived from "comb"-an archaic term for valley. I have also seen Combays who claimed to have been French, and there are even one or two Cumbys who claim to have come from Prussia. Cousin David Cumbia reported a family tradition that the name was Italian. Dr. Paul Comba, a well-known astronomer, an asteroid hunter, is from Italy, so Comba is evidently also an Italian name. The Combier (pronounced something like "Comb-e-ay") Distillery in France produces absinthe. A quick look at the Mormon page showed a few individuals named Cumba or Combay. What I have not seen is any credible ancestry with the name McCumbee. That name seems to have entered the family folklore due to some quick reading done by some relatives who did not do any actual research. There were and are people with names like McCumbee, but there is no evidence of any family connection between them and our ancestors.

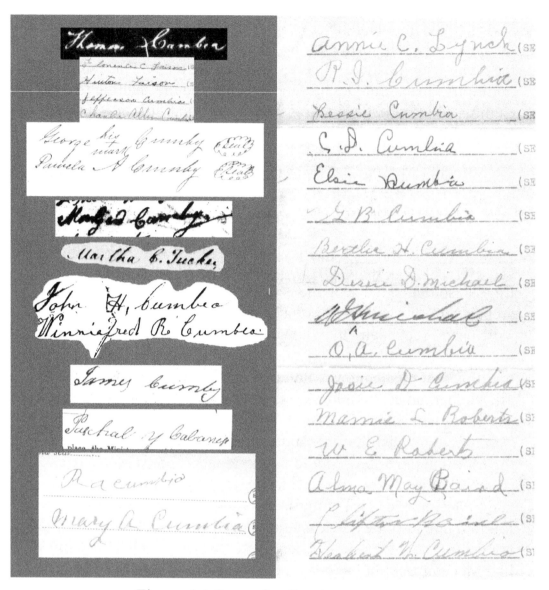

Figure 4.1 Some family signatures

134

Cemeteries

Studying records for Mecklenburg, Prince George, Pittsylvania, Dinwiddie, and Brunswick Counties, and elsewhere, I have devoted a considerable amount of labor toward finding the burial places of our ancestors (and our near contemporaries.)

Reverend John Weatherford is buried near Shockoe Baptist Church, near Chatham, Virginia. There are two Shockoe Baptist Churches, one white and one black. To go to the cemetery, take Rt. 832 away from Chatham, Virginia, then turn right on Rt. 640. Rev. Weatherford is not buried in the church cemetery. He is buried in a family cemetery a few hundred yards west of the church. The cemetery is down a dirt road behind the church, and it is in a field, recognizable in the distance by the trees that have grown up in it. Some local people have placed a marker where they believe Rev. Weatherford is buried. When I visited the gravesite in 2003 I walked aware that, if Gabriel blew his horn, Reverend Weatherford's eager leap toward Heaven might knock me down.

An overgrown family cemetery is near Adsit and Purdy in Brunswick County. It is very likely that John Henry's wife, Winnifred Thompson Cumbia, is buried there, but no marker exists at her grave. The cemetery cannot be seen from the road, and it is in thick, almost impenetrable woods. Jeff Finch, a local friend of the family, showed me the location, remembering that he had attended the burial of John Cumbia at that site. He thought that he had possibly witnessed the burial of John Henry Cumbia. We found instead the graves of Charles Henry's son, John A., and his wife, Ophelia Browder. Other people were also buried at the cemetery, including in laws named Dameron and Flint. An impressive stone obelisk has Flint on one side and Cumbia on the other. Individual graves are indicated only by depressions or field stones. Charles Henry Cumbia and his wife, Florence Flint, are probably buried there. It is unfortunate that so few of the graves are marked, and it is regrettable that the cemetery is in such a rundown condition.

Figure 4.2 Obelisk at Flint/Dameron/Cumbia cemetery

Figure 4.3 The Cumbia side of the Flint/Cumbia obelisk

Figure 4.4 Tombstone of John A. Cumbea

Figure 4.5 Grave marker for Ophelia Combia

Ophelia Cumbia's marker, beside John's, was knocked over and covered by a tree blown down by Hurricane Isabel. She was buried at the cemetery in 1963, only 43 years ago in 2006, which is a warning of what could happen to the home place cemetery in Brodnax if we are not careful.

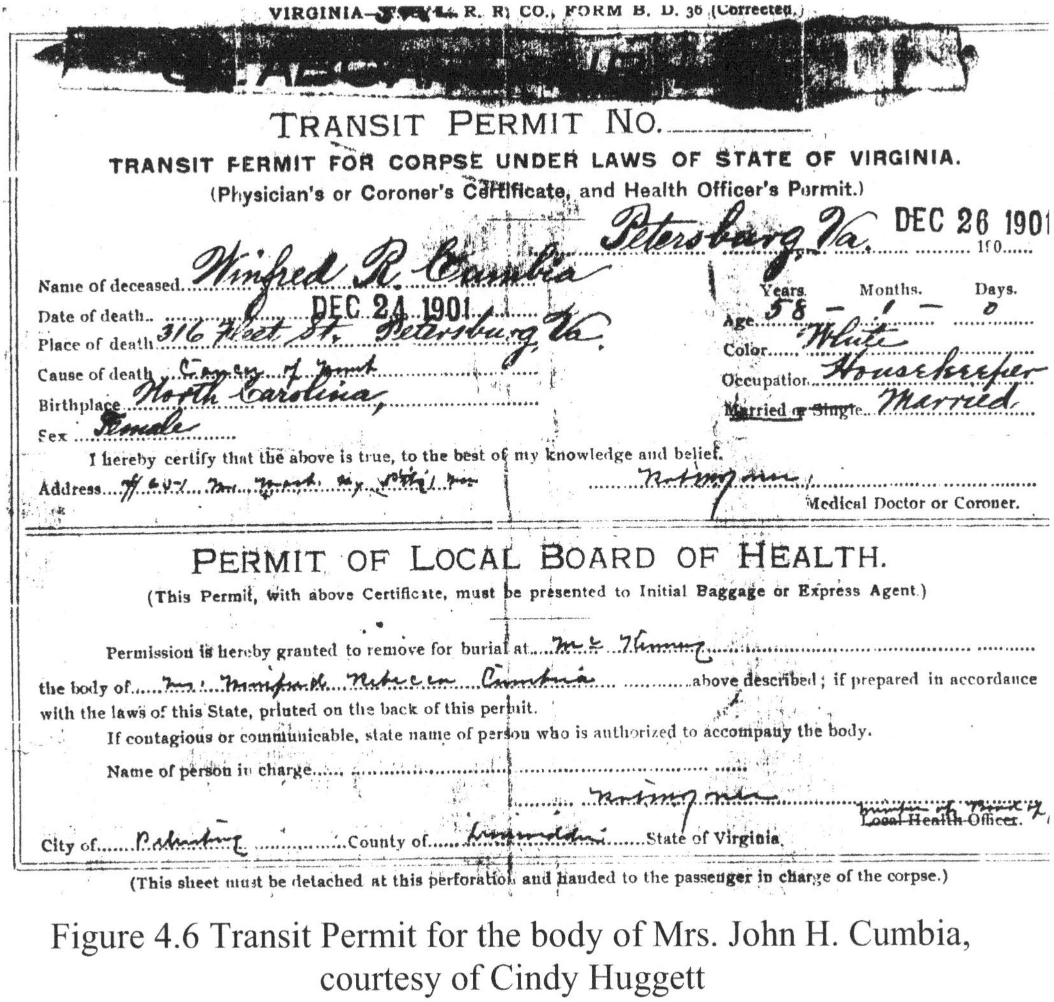

Figure 4.6 Transit Permit for the body of Mrs. John H. Cumbia, courtesy of Cindy Huggett

Figure 4.7 Dameron tombstones

John Henry Cumbia and his son Thomas Jonathon, with some other members of Thomas's family, are buried in Oakwood Cemetery on Nine Mile Road in Richmond, VA. John Henry's burial site was documented by Dorothy Cumbea, and I wasted some time looking for it because I had overlooked the location in her notes.

John Henry Cumbia's daughter, Harriett Early Pearson, is buried in Blandford Cemetery, beside her husband, William, and her sister, Emma. Major's first wife, Nancy B. Cumby, and a child named David Cumby, possibly a son of Major and Nancy, are also buried in Blandford Cemetery. They are buried in the Griffin plot where her son William is buried. The graves are not marked, but the Blandford staff can show you the location.

Although Charles Friend was not a blood relative, he figured prominently in the life of Major Weatherford Cumbea. It seems worth mentioning, therefore, that Mr. Friend is buried in the Blandford Cemetery. As perhaps an indication of hard times after the Civil War, Charles Friend's grave has no legible marker.

Carolyn Davis has shown me the location of a fairly large cemetery near where George and Thomas Cumby lived in Mecklenburg County. She pointed out that the cemetery is near an ancestral home of the Coley family. Only a few of the graves have markers, and there are no markers indicating Cumby graves. Still, this seems like the most likely place for poor neighbors in hard times to have been buried. Carolyn feels sure that some of our ancestors are buried there.

Edward Green Cumba, his wife Margaret, and their son Tom are buried in Sunset Memorial Park at Littleton, North Carolina.

I have followed up on several leads in the hope of finding the graves of Major and Adelia Cumbea, regrettably without success. I still hope to find their graves eventually, but so far I have not been able to do so. I suspect that they were not buried at Blandford because Nancy was buried there. Their graves seem likely to be lost in the land that once was their plantation, Palestine.

James Edward Cumbea, a son of Major and Adelia, is buried in Oakland Cemetery in Atlanta, Georgia.

Buried at Oakwood Cemetery in South Hill, Virginia, are Robert Ivan Cumbia, Sr., and his wife, Bessie Dawson Cumbia, Robert Ivan, Jr., his wife Frances Spence, their son, David George, and Dorothy Parker (Hortense), Robert and Bessie's daughter.

Alpheus Thomas Cumbia, Sr, and his wife, Kathleen, are buried at Providence United Methodist Church in Forksville, Virginia.

Otis Allen and Josie Cumbia and their son Joseph and his wife Ethel are buried at Crestview Memorial Park in South Hill, VA. Herbert and Nellie Cumbia and Norfleet and Ann Wilkerson Cumbia are also buried at Crestview.

Rev. Philip Cumbia is buried at Greenwood Memorial Gardens in Richmond, Virginia. Gilbert Cumbia is buried at Greenwood.

Dr. Jesse Cumbia, Philip's twin brother, is interred at Monticello Memory Gardens in Charlottesville, Virginia.

Otis Douglas Cumbia and his wife, Ruth, and their infant daughter, Mary Alice, are buried in LaCrosse, VA. Their daughter, Ruth Carolyn Snead, died in 2001 and is buried at Clover Cemetery. Gloria Cumbia Pulliam's husband, David Ray Pulliam, who died in 2001, is buried at Buffalo Baptist Church.

Wilson Abbitt Michael and his wife, Elizabeth Wesson (Biddie), are buried at Greensville Memorial Cemetery.

Wilford and Nancy Cumbia are buried at Westhampton Memorial Park in Richmond.

William Allen Cumbia, a son of John Henry and Winnifred Cumbia, his wife Rowena Abernathy, and their son, William, Jr., are buried in a Methodist churchyard in Edgerton, VA. W. Marvin Cumbia and Annie Owen Cumbia are also buried at the church at Edgerton.

Clarence David Cumbia, Sr., his wife Ritchie, and their son Bobby are buried at Mount Hope Cemetery in Rocky Mt., North Carolina.

The Cumbia family cemetery on the home place of Robert Allen and Mary Cumbia is the burial site for numerous family members. They include the following: Robert and Mary Cumbia, Charlie and Hattie Cumbia and their son Allen, Sue and George Lynch, Mamie and Eddie Roberts, Dessie and Harry Michael, George Burnice and Bertha Cumbia, Oscar and Althea Cumbia and their son Oscar Junior, my mother Louise Whitby, Evelyn and William Black, Gerald and Young Cumbia's son Christopher, and Megan and Caitlin Whitby, twin daughters of Uta and Sam Whitby. Miss Lucy Coley, an aunt of Mary Griffith's, is also buried in the Cumbia cemetery. Otis and Josie's infant daughter, Mildred Hortense, is buried there, as are the infants of Dessie and Sue.

Figure 4.8 Part of the Cumbia family cemetery in Brodnax, VA

Figure 4.9 Miss Mamie Cumbea, family connection unknown, from a
Post Card

Suggestions for further research

Due to limitations of time, all possible lines of the Cumbia ancestry were not studied in detail. Bloodlines exist or existed in Halifax, Charlotte, Campbell, Russell, Giles, Mecklenburg, Brunswick, and Appomattox Counties. In the 16 and 17 hundreds, probable ancestors lived in James City County, New Kent, Charles City, King George, and elsewhere. In some cases, a quick look at the data was enough to indicate ancestry and movement of the various lines. Simeon and his wife Aimey and Thomas and his wife Eliza, for example, moved from Campbell County and started branches of the Cumby family in Appomattox County. In other cases, there is still much work to be done before all the branches of the Cumbia family tree can be reliably charted.

For the branches that moved out of state, I have not had the time or resources to try to do the necessary research. For example, there were numerous people named Cumby in Texas before the Civil War. I strongly suspect, given that some of those people claimed to have been born in Virginia, kinship with our ancestors. George A. Cumby had at least three brothers, about whom we know almost nothing, and some or all of them could have moved out West. A researcher could make a big contribution to our knowledge of our ancestry by studying the family trees of the Texan Cumbys.

I have not read all the Chancery Court records for Halifax County. They may hold important clues. For example, Charles Cumbo died in about 1802, and the probate of his Will is among the Halifax records.

Some specific questions deserve further study. One would like to have more evidence for the identities of the parents of Thomas Cumby, George's father. It would be helpful if someone could find his death record, including the names of his parents, the date of death, and the place of his burial. What were the circumstances of the death of Agnes, Thomas's wife? And where was she buried? Some Weatherford researchers who have not answered my queries say that she died in childbirth. The existence of an Agnes Cumby in Campbell County, where George Cumby was born, leaves one with nagging doubts about whether or not we have identified the correct parents of George and Major. Did Thomas and Martha Cumby separate before Thomas's death? I would be glad to learn what happened to Catherine Cumby Pritchett (also called Pritchard) and her children, as well as what happened to Mary Susana Brooks and her family. Major Cumbea's farm was on the Confederate front line of the siege of Petersburg. It would be very interesting to learn more about life there during the Civil War. What happened to Mary, John, and Thomas Cumbea, the children of Major Weatherford and Nancy Cumbea? Where are the graves of Major and Adelia Cumbea? I would like to learn what happened to Major's slaves after Emancipation. More old family photographs may exist, and their discovery would be exciting. (I have been told that many wonderful photographs in Henry Cumbia's collection were simply thrown away.)There is plenty of work left to be done on the Cumbia family genealogy and history.

Footnotes

[i] http://www.familysearch.org/eng/default.asp

[ii] F http://ypng.infospace.com/info.whtpgs/wp/ .

[iii] Mecklenburg County Genealogy Project, http://www.rootsweb.com/~vameckle/index.htm.

[iv] Mec http://www.rootsweb.com/~vameckle/1870use.htm .

[v] Dr. William M. Pritchett, **Civil War Soldiers from Brunswick County, Virginia**, ed. John W. Pritchett

[vi] Weatherford Family, http://freepages.genealogy.rootsweb.com/~weatherford/.

[vii] Chesterfield Connections, Chesterfield County, Virginia, Sheriff's Office, http://chesterfield.gov/ConstitutionalOfficers/Sheriff/History.asp.

[viii] Faye Royster Tuck, **Yesterday-Gone Forever, A Collection of Articles**, quoted with permission of author, The Halifax County Historical Society.

[ix] Charles Friend, Papers, 1792-1871, 1839-1871, **The diaries and account book of Charles Friend**, also **Reminiscences of Jennie Friend**, Call Number Mss 1 F9156 at The Virginia Historical Society.

[x] Dr. William Scarborough, **The Overseer: Plantation Management in the Old South** (Baton Rouge, Louisiana State University Press, 1966), p. 48.

[xi] Jeffry C. Weaver, **The Virginia Regimental Histories Series** (Saltville, VA, Jeffrey C. Weaver, 2005).

[xii] John Worsham, **One of Jackson's Foot Cavalry**, http://docsouth.unc.edu/worsham/menu.html.

[Xiii] www.**combs**-families.org/**combs**/jhc/ms-jhc.html, "The Combes Genealogy" by Dr. Josiah H. **Combs**

[xiv] at http://etext.lib.virginia.edu/etcbin/ot2www-costa?specfile=/web/data/users/costa/costaslave.o2w&act=surround&offset=889883&tag=Runaway+Slave:+Virginia+Gazette+(Purdie+&+Dixon),+Williamsburg,+September+29,+1768.++&query=Cumbo .

[xv] Paul Heinegg, www.free**africanamericans**.com/, See entries on Cumbo family. See also *Free African Americans of North Carolina, Virginia, and South Carolina*.

[xvi] Martha W McCartney, *James City County, Keystone of the Commonwealth*, See esp. pp 258, 321, 490-492, 1997, The Downing Company Publishers.

A Few Final Words

Studying the Cumbia family tree has been great fun, but the fun must sooner or later come to an end. Although there is no end to questioning, there is an end to the documents that can be checked in a reasonable amount of time. There is a fine line between a hobby and a waste of time. One must turn back from history to the present. A lesson of recent events (this is being written in the wake of the terrorist attacks on the Pentagon and the Twin Towers of the World Trade Center) is that one should focus attention on kindness toward people in the present. Still, I hope these findings will be preserved and passed down to future generations. Maybe our descendants will have access to historical documents that we do not. Maybe they will be able to find answers where we have found only more questions. Maybe they can build upon our efforts and make the world a friendlier place.

Acknowledgements

I give thanks and gratitude to all of the people who helped compile this history of our ancestors. My mother, Louise Whitby, and her sister, Evelyn Black, provided invaluable encouragement and recollections. Noel Cumbia informed me about numerous web sites that were helpful. Cindy Huggett shared her research and sent photos that were wonderful. Carolyn Davis provided much information and an untiring interest in family history. My cousin, Angela Phillips, provided Family Tree Maker software. Dorothy Cumbea very generously sent about a hundred pages of her notes, including a carefully drawn family tree of her branch of the family. Several Cumby or Cumbie individuals generously talked to me and imparted their knowledge of their families, including Morris Cumby from Chesterfield County and Ethel Cumbie from Halifax County. Philip Cumbia informed me about his visit to Omega, Virginia, in Halifax in search of family history, and he encouraged our research at every opportunity. Steve Cumbea, Susan Lloyd, and Larry Mills – descendants of Major Weatherford Cumbea - sent me their findings and their photographs and their contagious interest in family history. Cousin Willie Munn provided documents, photographs, and a lot of much needed encouragement. Although Mr. Emmett Pulley has long been deceased, I remember his kind assistance with gratitude. Jeff Finch, who lives in Smoky Ordinary and who was a lifelong friend of Henry Cumbia, generously gave his time and braved a forest full of poison oak in order to guide me to a neglected family cemetery. He also shared much family lore and several photographs, saved not because of any biological relationship, but because of his affection and respect for the Cumbia family. David and Herschel Wells sent photographs and shared their enthusiasm. John Wells, co-author of *The Wellses of Mecklenburg County, Virginia*, sent me portions of that book and gave me helpful information about the Wells family. Brenda Cook and her son Bryon alerted us to the existence of

Worsham's "One of Jackson's Foot Cavalry." David Cumbia mailed a fine photograph of John Henry Cumbia, along with interesting and useful recollections. Wonderful family photos were provided by cousins Darlene Hinman and Kenny Michael and Robert and Gloria Cumbia . Kitty and Buford Cabaniss provided family lore and guided me to a Cabaniss family cemetery. The staff at the Library of Virginia and the staff of the Virginia Historical Society helped me with various problems. I first found the 1850 and 1870 Censuses and the 1870 Mecklenburg County map on the Internet page of VaGenWeb's Mecklenburg County Virginia Genealogy Project, coordinated by JoLee Gregory Spears. Paul Heinegg's research on early Cumbos was invaluable. He emailed his permission to quote from his work. I encourage those who are interested in the early history of the family to buy and read Heinegg's book. Special thanks go to our son, David Ray Whitby, who spent many hours with me at the Library of Virginia, patiently reading microfilmed records. He was the one who found several crucial documents, and his contribution is immense. David also made some helpful suggestions regarding the format of this book. Uta, my wife, has been very patient and encouraging while I did this research. Tyler Benjamin Whitby, my youngest son, has asked many questions that have motivated me to look for good answers. My father, Ray Whitby, helped me find useful photographs. I thank and ask forgiveness from my friend and co-worker, Blanche Herrington, who read this history and remarked that she "enjoyed it, but you included too many dates." Numerous people, some of whom were unrelated to the family, have read and constructively criticized my work, and I thank them. The mistakes are mine. To the relative who rejected my gift of this book with the comment that he was not interested in any dead Cumbias, I offer forgiveness and understanding. I love him anyway. Nobody owes enjoyment of this book to the author or anyone else, except maybe himself. To anyone I may have forgotten to mention, I apologize, assuring you that your assistance is very much appreciated.

MALES OF "OUR" CUMBO/CUMBIA LINE

EMMANUEL CUMBO
    LATE 1600S

RICHARD COMBOO

JOHN CUMBO

THOMAS CUMBO, SR
    D 1817

THOMAS CUMBY
B 1775 D AFTER 1850

GEORGE CUMBY / CUMBIA
1805-1884

ROBERT ALLEN CUMBIA
    1857-1935

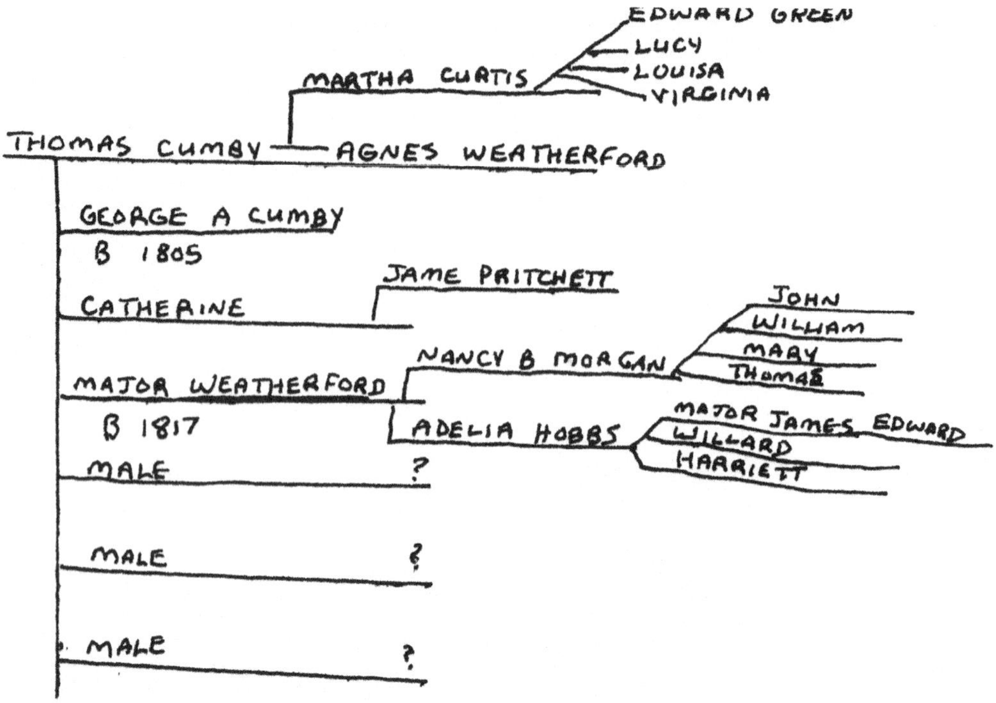

EDWARD GREEN
LUCY
MARTHA CURTIS
LOUISA
VIRGINIA

THOMAS CUMBY —— AGNES WEATHERFORD

GEORGE A CUMBY
B 1805

CATHERINE
JAME PRITCHETT

JOHN
WILLIAM
NANCY B MORGAN
MARY
THOMAS

MAJOR WEATHERFORD
B 1817
ADELIA HOBBS
MAJOR JAMES EDWARD
WILLARD
MALE ?
HARRIETT

MALE ?

MALE ?

GEORGE CUMBIA'S FAMILY

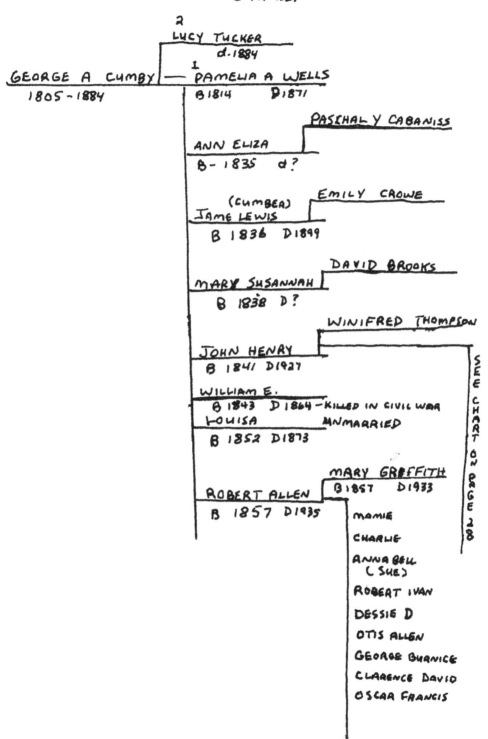

2
LUCY TUCKER
d. 1884

1
PAMELIA A WELLS
B 1814   D 1871

GEORGE A CUMBY
1805 - 1884

PASCHAL Y CABANISS

ANN ELIZA
B - 1835   d?

(CUMBEA)   EMILY CROWE
JAME LEWIS
B 1836   D 1899

DAVID BROOKS

MARY SUSANNAH
B 1838   D?

WINIFRED THOMPSON

JOHN HENRY
B 1841   D 1927

WILLIAM E.
B 1843   D 1864 - KILLED IN CIVIL WAR

LOUISA   UNMARRIED
B 1852   D 1873

MARY GRIFFITH
B 1857   D 1933

ROBERT ALLEN
B 1857   D 1935

MAMIE
CHARLIE
ANNABELL
(SUE)
ROBERT IVAN
DESSIE D
OTIS ALLEN
GEORGE BURNICE
CLARENCE DAVID
OSCAR FRANCIS

SEE CHART ON PAGE 28

Made in United States
North Haven, CT
16 March 2022

17218428R00089